Lau v. Nichols
Bilingual Education in Public Schools

Stephanie Sammartino McPherson

Landmark Supreme Court Cases

Enslow Publishers, Inc.

40 Industrial Road   PO Box 38
Box 398   Aldershot
Berkeley Heights, NJ 07922 Hants GU12 6BP
USA   UK

http://www.enslow.com

To Janis Sammartino, my sister, writing partner, and best friend

Copyright © 2000 by Stephanie Sammartino McPherson

Library of Congress Cataloging-in-Publication Data

McPherson, Stephanie Sammartino.
  Lau v. Nichols : bilingual education in public schools / Stephanie
Sammartino McPherson.
    p. cm. – (Landmark Supreme Court cases)
Includes bibliographical references and index.
Contents: Crisis in Chinatown—The Chinese Struggle for education—
The beginning of bilingual education—The case takes shape—The case
for the Chinese-speaking students—The case for the school district—
The Supreme Court decides—*Lau* v. *Nichols* changes education—Newest
challenge.
  ISBN 0-7660-1472-X
  1. Lau, Kinney Kinmon–Trials, litigation, etc.—Juvenile literature.
2. San Francisco (Calif.) Board of Education—Trials, litigation,
etc.—Juvenile literature. 3. Education, Bilingual—Law and
legislation—United States—Juvenile literature. 4. Chinese
students—Education—California—San Francisco—Juvenile literature.
[1. Lau, Kinney Kinmon—Trials, litigation, etc. 2. Education,
Bilingual—Law and legislation.] I. Title: Lau versus Nichols.
II. Title. III. Series.
  KF228.L278 M39 2000
  344.73'0791—dc21   00-008687

Printed in the United States of America

10 9 8 7 6 5 4 3 2

To Our Readers: We have done our best to make sure all Internet addresses in this book were active
and appropriate when we went to press. However, the author and the publisher have no control over
and assume no liability for the material available on those Internet sites or on other Web sites they
may link to. Any comments or suggestions can be sent by e-mail to comments@enslow.com or to the
address on the back cover.

Photo Credits: Courtesy of the Alice Fong Yu School Parent Teacher Association, p. 24;
Courtesy of Charles Barry, Santa Clara University, p. 45; Courtesy of the Department of
Elections, San Francisco, California, p. 103; Courtesy of Jonathan Gardner, pp. 59, 81, 85,
93, 101; Franz Jantzen, Collection of the Supreme Court of the United States, pp. 54, 109;
Harris and Ewing, Collection of the Supreme Court of the United States, p. 82; Joseph D.
Lavenburg, Collection of the Supreme Court of the United States, p. 86; National
Archives, pp. 18, 27, 36; San Francisco History Center, San Francisco Public Library,
pp. 7, 8, 16, 23, 42; Yochi R.Okamoto, Collection of the Supreme Court of the United
States, p. 78.

Cover Photo: John Henley/The Stock Market

Contents

Acknowledgments

Special thanks to Ling-Chi Wang, Edward Steinman, and Burk Delventhal for sharing their experience, knowledge, and memories of the *Lau* v. *Nichols* case.

I would also like to thank Janis Sammartino, Richard McPherson, Jennifer McPherson, Angelo Sammartino, and Jean Ramirez for their valuable suggestions.

For help in securing photographs, I am indebted to Selby Collins of the San Francisco History Center; Franz Jantzen and Curtis Miller of the Supreme Court Photo Archives; Susan Goldstein of the San Francisco Public Library; Kate Farrell of the San Francisco Unified School District; Naomi Nishioka of the San Francisco Department of Elections; and Liana Szeto, principal of Alice Fong Yu School.

A very big thank you to Jonathan Gardner for creating the graphic art and diagrams.

Author's Note

Can you imagine what it would be like to go to school in China and not to speak or understand Chinese? This book is about the struggles of Chinese children who attended California schools in the early 1970s but could not speak or understand English. The *Lau* v. *Nichols* lawsuit was an effort to establish their right to a meaningful education—one that would prepare them for successful futures in the United States. The landmark Supreme Court decision still touches the needs of thousands of non-English-speaking children in schools across the country.

1

Crisis in Chinatown

As a small child, Kinney Kinmon Lau knew little beyond the colorful neighborhood of San Francisco's Chinatown. Everything he and his mother needed was contained in the small space of a few miles—grocery stores, churches, businesses, and doctors' offices. There were even special schools that offered studies in Chinese language and culture. But these late-afternoon classes did not prepare children for life in the United States. And they did not take the place of the public schools the children attended each day.

Kinney did not have to think much about school until he turned six years old in 1969. That fall, his mother took him to Jean Parker Elementary School to start first grade. Like the other young people in the class, Kinney must have been curious, excited, and perhaps a little scared. But no adult could have comforted the little

5

boy or explained what would happen next. Kinney spoke no English; his teacher spoke no Chinese.

Widespread Dilemma

Kinney Lau was not alone in his confusion. Almost three thousand children in the San Francisco Unified School District spoke primarily Chinese.[1] That number had been rising since 1965, when Congress passed laws that opened the way for Chinese immigration to the United States.[2] Before that time, federal law had severely limited the number of Chinese people allowed into the United States. It was estimated that more than one thousand students newly arrived from China enrolled in San Francisco schools each year.[3] More than nine-tenths of them were not fluent in English.[4]

Frustrated and bored, these children sat in classrooms day after day. The younger students had little idea of what school was supposed to mean. Those who had attended school in China before coming to the United States had strong backgrounds in history, science, and math. Now, no one could teach them these subjects in Chinese. Meanwhile, they were not learning any English either. They had hit a brick wall in their learning.

Parents felt as powerless as their children. Most of them did not speak English themselves and had no way to communicate their dissatisfaction to school officials. Someone was needed to bridge the gap between the two groups. Ling-Chi Wang was neither a parent nor a school official. But the young graduate student from the University of California at Berkeley took a deep interest in the immigrants. He visited San Francisco's Chinatown and spoke with families in Chinese. "What I saw was widespread poverty and a lot of school children who were totally silenced because they didn't understand the language," Wang recalled.[5]

The "sink or swim" approach of immersing Chinese-speaking students in English-speaking classes and waiting to see what happened simply was not working. Too many Chinese children were sinking. Wang was disheartened to see young people giving up on school. Some became depressed; others turned defiant, dropping out and joining street gangs.[6] Eager to help the children, Wang started a committee to study the growing problem. He worked with social agencies, teachers, administrators, and adult

Kinney Lau went to Jean Parker Elementary School (shown here) when he started first grade in 1969.

Ling-Chi Wang was a graduate student from the University of California at Berkeley who took a deep interest in Kinney Lau and other immigrants like him. Ling-Chi Wang visited San Francisco's Chinatown (shown here) to speak personally with some of the families who spoke only Chinese.

immigrants. But for all his dedication, Wang had little to show for his efforts. Finally, in February 1969, Wang organized a large meeting between top school officials and the increasingly frustrated parents.

Violent Meeting

Commodore Stockton, the largest elementary school in San Francisco's Chinatown, was jammed with people. Seated on the stage, Superintendent Jenkins and the other officials looked out at a sea of Chinese parents and grand-parents and white schoolteachers. A number of rebellious-looking young people also sat in the audience. Ling-Chi Wang sensed the mounting tension as he trans-lated the questions and the answers.[7] Parents wanted to know why their children were not learning English or at least studying subjects in their native Chinese language. Officials responded with detailed analysis of the budget. To mothers and fathers desperately worried about their children's future, this seemed like no answer at all.

Unable to follow the involved financial reasoning, some people had even begun to doze off when the sound of an exploding firecracker alarmed everyone.[8] A number of hostile young people wearing buttons that read "Yellow Peril," had slipped into the back of the room. The slogan was intended to point out the anger of the young people in the audience. It both mocked the fears of the school officials and indicated that the youths, many of them gang members, were ready to fight for their rights.

9

Someone yelled that Chinese students were tired of hearing the same useless answers over and over again. Angry young men and women lining the rear wall backed the complaint with cries of "Right on!"[9]

All semblance of order disappeared as harsh insults and loud demands filled the room. An angry Chinese man leaped onto the stage, forcing a note on Superintendent Jenkins and demanding that he read it. But suddenly the superintendent was staring down at a firecracker that had hit his chest. If it exploded, he could be badly burned.

Without going off, the firecracker slid to the floor. Soon the defiant youths were throwing eggs and more firecrackers across the room. Ling-Chi Wang abruptly ended the meeting and began ushering the school officials out the doors behind the stage. One official found that his car had been set on fire.

What had gone wrong? The disastrous evening prompted Ling-Chi Wang to re-evaluate his methods. He had hoped that meetings and public discussions would bring Chinese parents and school officials closer together. Instead the gap between them was wider than ever. Wang no longer believed that discussion would benefit the children. The next step seemed clear to him—a lawsuit.[10]

A Lawyer Investigates

Edward Steinman, a young attorney, had met Ling-Chi Wang at several community meetings in Chinatown.

Steinman too was deeply interested in the welfare of thousands of Chinese children who could not speak English. He worked at the Chinatown office of the San Francisco Legal Assistance Foundation. "Literally everybody who was a client of mine had to have an interpreter," he recalled.[11] It seemed clear to Steinman that his clients' children did not know English either. Although they came to him for other matters like wage disputes, Steinman also began asking his clients how their children coped in school.

Candidly, parents explained the obstacles their children faced in class. Kinney's mother, Mrs. Kam Wai Lau, described her son's confusion and unhappiness in an English-speaking environment. Steinman was deeply disturbed. Surely, he thought, the school district could do more to help Kinney and other Chinese-speaking children. In fact, he was certain that federal law required it. He promised his clients he would look into the matter.[12]

Steinman went straight to the San Francisco Unified School District to get the facts he needed. A number of programs had been developed to help children who did not speak English. Some of the young people were taken out of regular classes forty minutes a day to study English as a second language, ESL, as the program was called, in the schools.[13] But over seventeen hundred students did not even receive this much help.

Like the people at the meeting, Steinman wanted more than numbers. He wanted to see for himself how individual children and teachers dealt with the language problem. At Commodore Stockton (today, Gordon Lau) Elementary School, site of the violent meeting, he visited several classes and found the teachers unable to communicate with many of the students. Bored and unhappy, the children simply marked time in the classroom. They could not understand instructions or ask any of the dozens of questions they must have had.

Steinman still had many questions of his own. He continued to ask his clients about their children. All the parents he met thought the schools should be doing more to help Chinese-speaking youngsters. Not only was there no written material available in Chinese, there were very few bilingual (Chinese- and English-speaking) teachers. Some observers felt that the school district actually discriminated against Chinese teachers. One writer summed up the prevailing prejudice, "Chinese are not good teachers because they have an accent, they lack initiative, they are too soft-spoken, bilingual teachers are not effective in any subject."[14]

For years, the Chinese community in San Francisco had worked to change such offensive and false beliefs. But for all their protests, Steinman knew that the Chinese Americans were politically powerless. The school district itself admitted that its budget to help children who did not speak English was "woefully inadequate."[15]

By the time they were teenagers, many Chinese students had decided that school was not worth the bother. Dropout rates soared, and so did juvenile delinquency. Unable to find jobs, many former students turned to petty crime. In school or out, they had nothing to look forward to. Like Wang, Steinman wanted to stop this cycle of failure. If only they could persuade the school board to address the problems of the Chinese-speaking children, more of them might be motivated to graduate. The students could have realistic goals and promising futures.

President Alan Nichols and the other school board members listened carefully to Steinman's concerns. They agreed that the children he described needed help. But they did not agree to change anything. It was a matter of priorities, they explained. Many other children (including other language-minority students) also had special needs. Not all these needs could be met immediately. Some groups would simply have to wait. Although the board wanted to do more for the Chinese-speaking children, its members believed they were under no legal obligation to do so.[16]

Edward Steinman was not so sure about that. He believed the students had rights and the schools had responsibilities. But the school board would not budge from its position. Disappointed, Steinman discussed the situation with Ling-Chi Wang. The two agreed that a lawsuit should be filed. "I didn't know what else to do," Steinman said.[17]

13

2

The Chinese Struggle for Education

What to do about their children's education had long been an issue for Chinese workers living in California. Ever since the mid-1800s, when the first wave of Chinese immigration to the United States began, the newcomers had faced discrimination. In many places, only white children were permitted to attend public schools. The Chinese community wanted the same rights for its children that European immigrants enjoyed. But even when the San Francisco School Board did agree to provide for Chinese young people, the Chinese students were placed in a separate school.[1]

Things went from bad to worse when, in 1871, a new California education law totally ignored the Chinese population. Chinese children no longer had a legal right to any education at all. This meant their modest gains were gone. Almost at once the Chinese school was shut down. The school superintendent claimed that most days only about twenty students attended anyway. He did not want to spend money on them that could be spent educating white children.[2]

Treaty of Burlingame

School officials did not seem bothered by the fact that their actions violated an international agreement. In 1868, the United States and China had signed the Treaty of Burlingame. Each country had promised to respect the educational privileges of the other country. United States citizens in China could count on going to school, and Chinese immigrants in the United States were supposed to have the same right. But this was not the case in California.

Meanwhile, some people were working to change school regulations in that state. In 1880, the word "white" was taken out of the California Education Code. "Every school, unless otherwise provided by law, must be open for the admission of all children. . . ." read the revised document.[3] This should have been good news for the Chinese immigrants. Legally, there was nothing to prevent their children from entering school. But prejudiced school officials continued to find ways to keep Chinese young people out of the public schools.[4] Parents took their complaints to school boards and to the state lawmakers, but nothing changed.

Tape v. Hurley

Finally, in 1885, the parents of Mamie Tape, a child of mixed Chinese and Caucasian heritage, took the school system to court. Jennie Hurley, the principal of Spring Valley School, was listed as the defendant because she had denied Mamie entrance into the school.[5]

In *Tape* v. *Hurley*, the judge ruled against the school district, citing the Fourteenth Amendment to the Constitution. "No state shall make or enforce any law

San Francisco's Oriental School (shown here) kept Chinese children apart from other students in the city's school system. Mamie Tape's parents disagreed with this separation and took the school system to court.

which shall abridge the privileges or immunities of citizens of the United States . . . nor deny to any person within its jurisdiction the equal protection of the laws."[6] The message was clear. Mamie Tape was a citizen; she had the right to attend school. The ruling was upheld by the state Supreme Court.

Still the school board did not enroll Mamie in a school with white children. A separate school, the Chinese Primary School, was opened for her. Mamie's mother was furious. "Dear Sirs," she wrote to members of the school board, "Will you please tell me! Is it a disgrace to be Born a Chinese? Didn't God make us all!!!. . . . Just because she is descended of Chinese parents I guess she is more of an American than a good many of you that is going to prewent [prevent] her being Educated."[7] Mrs. Tape's letter appeared in the newspaper, but the school board refused to reconsider its position.

The Chinese Exclusion Act

By the 1880s, there were more than seventy-five thousand people of Chinese ancestry living in California.[8] They mined for gold, built railroads, worked in factories, and farmed. Many Americans resented these people for taking away jobs. Racial prejudice grew so strong that in 1882 Congress passed the Chinese Exclusion Act to slow the flow of immigrants into the United States. For ten years Chinese people were banned from settling in this country. Those people who had already immigrated were declared

By the 1880s, there were more than seventy-five thousand people of Chinese ancestry living in California. They mined for gold, built railroads, worked in factories, and fished. The Chinese fishermen shown here are drying shrimp and mending nets in the late 1800s.

ineligible for citizenship. Objections and protests from the Chinese population proved useless. In 1892, the act was renewed. Three years later the Native Sons of the Golden State (later called the Chinese-American Citizens Alliance) was created. Members declared themselves ready "to challenge any discrimination which may arise because of race and color."[9] But their efforts did not prevent the Exclusion Act from being renewed in 1902.[10]

The Right to Attend Neighborhood Schools

Congress had made it clear that Chinese people were not welcome in the United States. San Francisco continued to make it known that Chinese children were not welcome in the city schools either. The Chinese Primary School went only through fifth grade. As Chinese children completed their studies, they had no place to go but the regular high schools attended by white students. In 1900, however, the school board decided that Chinese students should remain separated in their own school—even when they had finished the fifth-grade work. Although the Chinese Primary School was not equipped to teach higher levels, Chinese students in city high schools were told to leave at once.

The entire Chinese community was furious. Chinatown newspapers urged parents to boycott the Chinese Primary School if their children were not allowed to proceed on to high school. The school board sensed danger. The whole city school system might have to be reorganized if the Chinese School was not used. Finally, school officials said that Chinese students could attend high school with white students.[11]

The next step was to get children into neighborhood elementary schools instead of making them attend a separate school. Wong Him, a doctor, decided to send his daughter to Clement School near one of his offices. At first, there was no problem. Katie was enrolled in class with all the other children. Then on March 1, 1902, the principal told Katie that she would have to leave the school.

Dr. Him saw no reason to take his daughter all the

way to the school in Chinatown. He filed a lawsuit stating that his daughter had rights as an American citizen. Dr. Him pointed out that American Indian, African-American, and Japanese-American children were all allowed into the regular public schools. Only the Chinese were forced to send their children to a separate facility.[12]

The court upheld the school district's right to maintain different schools for different races as long as the schools were equal. Dr. Him had not claimed the Chinese school was inferior to other schools. The court might have considered such an argument more favorably. Instead it ruled that Katie's rights were not being violated. As long as the Chinese school existed, that was the school she must attend.[13]

Chinese merchants were determined to change the law. They believed their children should have the right to attend any school in the city. No matter what the court said, it was not fair for Chinese children to be separated and put into a single school. "We Chinese are heavy taxpayers and we do not propose to put up with this state of affairs any longer. Why should we contribute to the support of public schools from which the native-born children of Chinese parents are excluded?"[14] Despite parents' efforts to get their children into regular schools, the answer was always the same. The school board did not believe that Chinese children should study and play with white children.

The Best Way to Learn English

Through the years, a few Chinese parents did manage to send their children to regular schools. Some principals were willing to admit Chinese students if white parents did not protest.[15] But by 1917, many Chinese children were still isolated in their own school. The original building had been destroyed in the San Francisco Earthquake of 1906. It had been rebuilt and renamed the Oriental School, but little else had changed. When the United States Commissioner of Education came to San Francisco to study the schools, he was especially interested in the Oriental School. He wanted to see how immigrant children were fitting in with American life.

With the commissioner watching, the students in one classroom were asked to stand up and say the Pledge of Allegiance. The commissioner listened carefully as the children stood and recited. Of course, the commissioner knew the pledge, but he could not understand the children's words. Their sounds were flat and slurred together as if they did not know where one word ended and the next began. Did they really understand the meaning of what they said? At his request, the teacher asked several children to explain the pledge. No one could. In fact, some children did not know English at all.[16] The visitor concluded that the students should be having special help with English. But their teachers, who did not speak Chinese, taught the same way as all the other teachers in the district.

21

If Chinese-speaking children went to school with native English speakers, they might learn the language more quickly, one educator pointed out. They would hear other children speaking English, and they would learn social customs and traditions. Separated in their own school, they did not speak English to each other very much. When they did, they often reinforced each other's mistakes in grammar and pronunciation.[17]

It was not until the late 1920s, however, that neighborhood schools were opened to Chinese children. By then the Oriental School, which had been renamed Commodore Stockton, was so crowded that it could not accept any more students. Other schools had to take them in. Two schools near the edge of Chinatown, Washington Irving and Jean Parker, were the first to admit Chinese youngsters.[18] Much later Kinney Lau would attend Jean Parker School.

Determined Young Girl

Growing up in the early 1900s, Chinese children in San Francisco faced racial prejudice as well as language problems. Alice Fong (later Alice Fong Yu), who was born in 1905, recalled her childhood vividly. A bright little girl, she was often snubbed and left out of activities. "[Non Chinese children] would make us cry coming home," she recalled years later. "Kids were very cruel to tell you things, and when game time came, they wouldn't hold our hands or let us play with them. So we just hung around by ourselves feeling very badly."[19]

Thanks to supportive parents and her own determination, Fong grew up to be an ambitious young woman with high goals. But when she applied for a teacher's program in San Francisco, she encountered more discrimination. "This lady wants to become a teacher?" commented one faculty member. "Oh no, I wouldn't advise it because she wouldn't be able to get a job; who would hire her?"[20] Only when Fong explained that she

It was not until the late 1920s that neighborhood schools in San Francisco were opened to Chinese children like the ones shown here who are learning about Chinese New Year.

A school in San Francisco was named in honor of Alice Fong Yu, many years later. The outside of the building includes Chinese characters.

planned to return to China to teach was she accepted in the course of study.

Alice Fong never returned to China after all. Instead, she changed her plans and, in 1926, became the first Chinese-speaking teacher hired by the San Francisco school district. Fong was sent to teach at the all-Chinese Commodore Stockton. "Their American teachers didn't understand [the students]," she remembered.[21] They continuously interrupted Fong's class, asking her to tell a child what to do or to remind a child what to bring to school the next day.

Short explanations in Chinese were one thing. But actually teaching in Chinese was an entirely different matter. "We weren't supposed to talk Chinese in the class," said Fong. "They specifically told me not to use it."[22]

Almost fifty years later most Chinese-speaking youngsters still were not hearing their native language in the classroom.

3

The Beginning of Bilingual Education

The Chinese were not the only ethnic group that had to overcome a language problem. But few other immigrant groups suffered the discrimination that the Chinese did. As early as colonial times, the children of Dutch, German, Swedish, and French settlers often established their own schools.[1] Not only did these young people learn to read and write in their native language, they studied geography, history, and arithmetic in it as well. No law said that they had to go to school at all. But most colonists agreed on the importance of learning. It was the only way to make sure that their traditions and culture survived in the new land.[2]

Educating a New Nation

After the Revolutionary War (1775–1783), Americans became even more focused on school issues.[3] If the new nation was to thrive, citizens needed to be well informed and educated. Nineteenth century reformers believed that all children should attend elementary school. Calling themselves "friends of education," they asked for state governments to supervise a system of common schools.[4] This system would provide young people with a basic education and promote democratic ideals. From big cities in the East to pioneer settlements in the West, common schools would teach the value of hard work, self-discipline, and patriotism. They would guarantee that all children knew what it meant to be American.

Being American did not necessarily mean speaking English. The United States has never adopted an official language.[5] In fact, some early patriots wanted to emphasize the new nation's independence by getting rid of English entirely. Why not speak German or French? some Americans asked. What about Hebrew or Greek? proposed others.[6] But too many people spoke English to make such suggestions practical. Noah Webster, who wrote the popular dictionary, believed that one day, "North America will be peopled with hundred of millions of men, all speaking the same language."[7] The language he was referring to was English.

One Nation, Many Languages

Meanwhile many languages continued to be spoken. The nineteenth century was a time of great growth for the United States. Between 1840 and 1924, 37 million immigrants poured into the country.[8] Although they wanted their children to adapt to new ways and learn the new language, many immigrants wanted them to remember their first language and culture too. German Catholics and Lutherans, devout in their religion, felt especially strongly about this. They believed that religious schools taught in German would help preserve their heritage. In their native language, they could make sure their children understood the basics of religion. "Language saves faith," they liked to remind each other.[9]

By the 1850s, German schools, both public and private, had spread from Baltimore to Milwaukee.[10] Ohio approved teaching in German for children whose parents wanted them fluent in their native language. In

Between 1840 and 1924, 37 million immigrants, people from many different countries who were looking for a new life, came to the United States. Immigrants arriving at Ellis Island in the late nineteenth and early twentieth century often spoke little or no English.

Louisiana, French was a widespread language; in the New Mexico territory, Spanish was spoken. These regions also provided for bilingual education. That meant that students studied their subjects in both English and the language they spoke at home. In various areas, schools offered classes for immigrant children in Polish, Italian, Norwegian, and Dutch.[11]

A conflict was beginning to develop. Supporters of the common school movement believed that immigrant children needed to forget their "old ways" in order to adopt American culture and values. But many parents felt their ethnic traditions and beliefs, their arts and languages, were worth remembering. Their children did not have to talk and look and think like everyone else in order to be good Americans.[12]

Conflict Erupts

In April 1917, the United States entered World War I against Germany. Suddenly German Americans found themselves under a great deal of suspicion. To some people, the Germans' desire to speak their own language seemed disloyal, even sinister.[13] A federal law was passed making it illegal to publish anything about the war in a foreign language. Within a year, twenty-five states outlawed the teaching of German in school.[14] Some places even banned the speaking of German at all. In the frenzy to erase the "enemy" language from America, restaurant owners made new menus. Instead of German fried potatoes or sauerkraut, diners were offered the same foods renamed American fries and liberty cabbage.[15]

Meyer v. Nebraska

Prejudice against the German language continued even after the war. But despite state laws, Robert T. Meyer, a Nebraska school teacher, continued to teach part-time in German. On May 25, 1920, he was reading Bible stories in German with a dozen fifth-graders. The other forty students sat silently at their desks reading in English. Suddenly, the class was interrupted by a surprise visitor. Frank Edgerton was a county attorney sent to investigate Meyer's teaching. Instantly Meyer had to make a decision. "I knew that, if I changed into English language, he would say nothing," Meyer told his lawyer. "If I went on in German, he would . . . arrest me. I told myself that I must not flinch. And I did not flinch. I went on in German."[16]

Convicted by the state and federal appeals courts in Nebraska, Meyer took his case all the way to the United States Supreme Court. In a seven to two vote, the Justices dismissed the state's argument that German language instruction encouraged children to have ideas "foreign to the best interests of this country."[17] Announcing the decision on June 4, 1923, Justice James C. McReynolds stated, "No emergency has arisen which renders knowledge by a child of some language other than English so clearly harmful as to justify its inhibition [a ban against teaching it] with the consequent infringement [lessening] of rights long freely enjoyed."[18] Once again, schools were free to teach in German.

But enrollment in German classes never came close to what it had been. In 1915, before World War I, about one quarter of all students studied German in high school. Seven years later the number had dropped to less than one percent.[19] The right to learn German was re-established, but much of the interest was gone.

The American Melting Pot

The pressure to "Americanize" immigrants gained strength after the war. So did prejudice against newcomers and a fear that foreign customs would somehow pollute the culture of the United States. In 1924, Congress passed an immigration act. The new law limited the number of people accepted into the country each year. New arrivals, quick to sense the general disfavor, felt handicapped by their differences. The young generation soon learned that the way to succeed was to give up old ways. The more they looked, acted, and spoke like other Americans, the better off they would be.[20] Often the United States was called a "melting pot," where differences were supposed to melt away as immigrants accepted American customs.

In a way, schools were supposed to be melting pots too. The bilingual educational programs of earlier days were rapidly fading. Most immigrant children were sent to school conducted entirely in English. One early-twentieth-century observer put it bluntly. The typical immigrant parent, he said, sent his children to school as "little Poles or Italians or Finns, babbling in the tongues of their parents, and at the end of half a dozen years or more he sees them emerge looking, talking, thinking and behaving generally like full-fledged Americans."[21]

But often children lost more than they gained. Although some young people grasped the language readily and did well, many children were confused and frightened. They could not learn in a language they did not understand. What they did understand clearly was that their parents' language and culture were not valued in the public schools.

This was a lesson that American Indians and Hispanics already knew too well. American-Indian children growing up in the late nineteenth century were sent to boarding schools where they were not allowed to speak in their tribal languages at all. If they were caught talking to each other in a language other than English, they were punished. Robert Lewis, an American Indian who became a state governor, recalled his student days vividly:

> When we wanted to speak our language we had to sneak off somewhere and get together as a group and talk to our heart's content. . . . I forgot my language because I went to boarding school when I was six. I mean the way of speaking it. I understood clearly whatever was spoken to me. When my parents or grandparents would come to meet me, I would

understand them and be able to greet them, but since I could not speak I would get embarrassed and run away. . . . I had to relearn the language.[22]

Spanish-speaking children in Texas and California were also denied instruction in their native language. Both states had strict English-only laws for school districts.[23] Even on the playground, children had to be careful. When teachers caught them speaking Spanish, they were kept after school.[24]

The Nation Takes Note

A few educators realized that forbidding children to speak their own language did not help them learn English. But it was not until the 1960s that bilingual education again became an issue in the United States. After Fidel Castro took over Cuba in 1959, many people seeking an escape from his Communist government fled to the United States and settled in Florida. In their own country, many of these Cubans had held important positions. Some had been teachers and other professionals. Determined to pass on their Hispanic heritage to their children, they made their voices heard. In 1963, Coral Way Elementary School in Dade County began a bilingual program not only for Spanish-speaking children, but also for English-speaking young people. Both sets of students benefited. "The pupils in Coral Way . . . are learning to operate effectively in two languages and two cultures," school officials concluded in 1966.[25]

That same year, the National Education Association (NEA) investigated a different situation that existed in Tucson, Arizona. Children who spoke Spanish received no English classes and were not taught any subjects in their native language. They were learning almost nothing in school. At a conference, NEA leaders called their situation to the attention of two United States senators. The NEA leaders introduced the politicians to teachers who thought that bilingual education might solve the children's problems.

According to language historian James Crawford, the Tucson convention "marked the [political] birth of the 'bilingual movement.' "[26] Educators and politicians all over the country began to study the problems of limited-English-proficiency (LEP) children. They began to realize their responsibility to students who spoke little or no English. New Mexico, which had generally been sensitive to the needs of Spanish-speaking children, passed a law that stated classes could be taught in languages besides English. Other states quickly followed suit. Massachusetts was the first state to go one step farther. Instead of merely allowing schools to offer bilingual education, it required them to do so when enough students needed the instruction.[27]

Finally, in 1968, Congress passed the Bilingual Education Act to help children who both were poor and did not speak English well. Now states could apply for federal funds to create school programs, train teachers, and get parents involved in their children's education. Schools were also encouraged "to impart to students a knowledge of the history and culture associated with their languages."[28] Instead of trying to "melt" away differences, schools were to teach that Americans came from many different backgrounds and should be proud of their heritage.

Brown v. Board of Education

While language minorities were struggling in school, African Americans faced their own battles for justice. Shortly after the Civil War, the Thirteenth Amendment to the Constitution prohibited slavery, and the Fourteenth Amendment gave citizenship to all former slaves. No state was allowed to take away their rights, freedom, or possessions except by law. In spite of these Fourteenth Amendment guarantees, almost one hundred years later, African Americans were still forced to live in separate neighborhoods and to send their children to separate schools. On buses and trains, in parks and restaurants, they were isolated. The civil rights movement challenged the laws and practices that violated African Americans' constitutional safeguards. Eventually, principles of equality established as a result of this movement would benefit children of limited English skills, too.

Like many African-American parents, the Browns of Topeka, Kansas, were unhappy with the school their daughter Linda was required to attend. Linda went to an all-black school twenty-one blocks from her home. The white elementary school, only five blocks from her home, was more modern and spacious, and it had many more teachers. However, state law prevented Linda from attending this school.

The Browns wanted the best for their daughter. They believed she had a right to attend the well-equipped school that was closer to her home. After talking it over and consulting with lawyers, the Browns decided to sue the school board. A federal judge for the United States District Court in Kansas ruled in favor of the school system. He stated that the United States Constitution permitted separate schools as long as they were equal. Even though Linda's school lacked up-to-date facilities and too many children were crowded into the classrooms, the judge declared that the schools were almost equal.

"Almost equal" was not good enough for the Browns. Neither was "separate." They took the case all the way to the United States Supreme Court. In 1954, the Justices were unanimous in overturning the ruling of the lower court. "[In] the field of public education the doctrine of 'separate but equal' has no place," stated Chief Justice Earl Warren. "Separate educational facilities are inherently unequal."[29]

The Supreme Court had established an important principle—one that invalidated the decision made years ago against Dr. Wong Him and his daughter. There was to be no segregation in the school system. All children, regardless of race or ethnic background, had the same right to an education. Later this principle would also

The *Brown* v. *Board of Education* case in 1954 clearly stated that the idea of "separate but equal" had no place in public education. The civil rights movement soon emerged, demanding equal education and opportunities for children of all races.

prove relevant to children who spoke little or no English. Language barriers were also a form of segregation, lawyers would argue. Children who could not talk to their teachers or classmates were not getting an equal education.

The Civil Rights Act of 1964

Another development that affected non-English-speaking children was the Civil Rights Act of 1964. Under Title VI of the new law, Congress declared, "No person in the

United States shall, on the ground of race, color, or national origin, be excluded from participation in, be denied the benefits of, or be subjected to discrimination under any program or activity receiving federal financial assistance."[30] Simply put, this meant that the government would not give funds to any organization or educational program that practiced discrimination.

The Department of Health, Education, and Welfare (HEW), now called the Department of Health and Human Services, was responsible for seeing that the new law was put into effect. Officials realized that language discrimination was a problem facing many children whose "national origins" differed from the majority of Americans. In 1970, the department published an order directing school districts to "take affirmative steps to rectify English language deficiencies which have the effect of excluding national origin minority children from participation in the educational program offered."[31] In other words, schools had to help children who did not speak English. Those students could not be left out of activities and classroom participation because they did not understand what was going on. If the schools disobeyed this order, any funds they received from the government would be stopped.

Court Battle in San Francisco

When Edward Steinman spoke with Mrs. Lau and members of other Chinese-speaking families, he knew that the

San Francisco school district received federal funds. He also knew that a language barrier separated Kinney and other Chinese-speaking youngsters from a normal educational experience. Kinney could not talk with English-speaking youngsters or share in their learning. He could not understand the stories the teacher read or follow her explanations when she talked about numbers. Steinman believed the school district was not entitled to any federal funds unless it met the needs of the Chinese-speaking population.

Both sides agreed that the Chinese-American children would benefit from special instruction in English. But while Steinman wanted to protect the students' civil rights, the school board wanted the right to develop its own priorities. Meanwhile, Kinney Lau and the other children were growing up. Their parents did not want them to miss out on more years of education. They wanted change immediately.

4

The Case Takes Shape

Edward Steinman knew how Chinese Americans felt about their children's classroom experience. Now he needed to gauge their feelings about a lawsuit.[1] Did they agree this was the right way to help their children? Did they fear that legal proceedings would make future cooperation with the school system impossible? Steinman spoke with as many Chinese parents as possible. He discussed the school district's obligations and what a lawsuit might accomplish for the children.

The parents listened carefully. Although they did not urge Steinman to proceed at once, they said nothing to discourage him either.[2] Steinman understood their caution. This was a big step for parents who had long felt powerless in the schools. But Steinman sensed they wanted him to do everything possible to help their children. With the school system refusing to budge, that meant a lawsuit.

Class Action Suit

Steinman's research revealed some twenty-eight hundred Chinese students of limited English ability in San Francisco.[3] Almost all of these children would benefit from a winning lawsuit. But not all the children would be named in the action that Steinman brought against the school district. He would choose several children to represent all the Chinese-speaking students in a class action suit. This is a legal proceeding brought by a small number of people (plaintiffs) on behalf of a larger group. Individuals not listed in the lawsuit, but who share a common problem with the plaintiffs, are part of the group. In this case, every Chinese-speaking child who was not getting sufficient help with English was part of the class action lawsuit. All of them, whether listed or not, would be bound by the court's decision.

Two Groups of Plaintiffs

Steinman's next step was to decide which children to name in the class action suit. He wanted a good sampling of youngsters in the district—boys and girls of various ages who attended several different schools. He also wanted children whose personal stories would appeal to the court. For example, first-grader Kinney Lau was an only child whose widowed mother worked long hours at a low-paying job to support him. He was a child certain to evoke the court's sympathy. Steinman listed Kinney Lau first among the plaintiffs.

Carefully going through school records and talking with parents, Steinman chose other children to be named in the lawsuit. These students were divided into two groups of plaintiffs. Neither group could speak or write English. The first group of plaintiffs got no special help in English at all. The second group of plaintiffs attended special classes part-time, but their teachers spoke no Chinese. The children were expected to understand explanations in English before they had actually mastered English. Besides Kinney, Steinman selected eight students, ages six to fourteen, to represent the first class of plaintiffs. The four students chosen to represent the second class of petitioners ranged in age from six to eleven.

Defendants

Who were the people responsible for the plaintiffs' situation? In the lawsuit, Steinman had to name all the people who made the decisions for the school district. They were the ones with the power to create more programs to help the Chinese-speaking children. As defendants (those who must answer charges in court), Steinman listed all members of the Board of Education, beginning with its president Alan H. Nichols. Steinman also named members of the board of supervisors of the city and county of San Francisco since they were legally in

As president of San Francisco's school board, Alan Nichols was cited as the first defendant in the lawsuit filed on behalf of the Chinese-speaking children of San Francisco.

charge of the elementary and high schools. Dr. Robert E. Jenkins, superintendent of the San Francisco Unified School District, was also cited as a defendant.

The Children Prepare

By December 1969, the lawsuit was a reality. To prepare the young plaintiffs for what would happen, Steinman invited all the children and their parents to his office.[4]

The young people munched cookies and met each other for the first time. With the help of an interpreter, Steinman told the children that sometimes when people disagree they go to court to settle their differences. There were two sides to the issue. On one side, the children's parents felt the schools were not teaching them what they needed to know. On the other, the school officials had no plans to change anything in the classrooms. The court would decide which side was right according to the law or whether the current law had to be changed. If the children's side won, they would learn to speak English in school. Then they would be ready to study new things and face new situations confidently. The children listened quietly and watched their parents sign the documents that marked the beginning of the lawsuit.

Usually the plaintiffs in a lawsuit must testify in court. They explain their complaint and tell why the defendants should be forced to meet their demands. But the children in *Lau* v. *Nichols* spoke no English and many were young enough to be easily intimidated by the formal courtroom procedure. Instead of asking them to testify before a judge, Steinman helped each of the plaintiffs to write a declaration.[5] With the help of a translator, each child described what school was like for him or her. Steinman wrote down their exact words as evidence that children do not learn when they cannot understand the language. The declarations also showed the frustration and unhappiness the children experienced at school.

The Case in District Court

Steinman and Wang worked closely together in developing the case.[6] Armed with the children's own words and seven arguments (causes of action) against the school district, Steinman filed a lawsuit on March 23, 1970, in the United States District Court for Northern California. Because the children were being taught in a language they did not understand, Steinman claimed that their right to an education was being violated. He declared that "such a fundamental right to education is guaranteed by the Constitution of the United States, the Constitution of the State of California, and laws enacted by the California State Legislature."[7] Steinman also asserted that the district's acceptance of federal funds obligated it to provide programs for all language-minority students. If corrective measures were not taken at once, the children would "suffer irreparable injury."[8]

It was up to school officials to defend their policy against the plaintiffs' charges. Thomas O'Connor, city attorney of San Francisco, and Raymond Williamson, Jr., deputy city attorney, represented the defendants. Immediately, they began gathering evidence of the district's commitment to its Chinese-speaking students. Both sides began the legal process known as discovery. This is the fact-finding procedure through which the plaintiffs and defendants can ask questions and demand information from each other. That way there are no

Edward Steinman (shown here many years after *Lau* v. *Nichols* was decided) filed a lawsuit on March 23, 1970, in the United States District Court for Northern California. He was seeking a means to educate the Chinese-speaking children of San Francisco.

surprises in court. Each side has a firm grasp of the material that is important to the case.

Both sides agreed on certain basic facts—that 2,856 Chinese-speaking children needed special help and that only 1,066 of these students were getting that help.[9] Even in the second group, most children were not getting all the assistance they required. Six hundred thirty-three children studied language only part-time, while four hundred thirty-three received full-time language instruction.[10]

In court, the defendants vigorously denied the plaintiffs' claims. Acknowledging that the school district did receive government funds to establish a Chinese bilingual program, they said that as many children were served as possible. Assistant Superintendent Isadore Pivnick explained that accepting funds did not require the school system to provide special classes for all the Chinese children in the school system. There was not enough money for that. Rather, certain schools were chosen based on the economic needs of the children's parents and evaluation of the students' language skills.[11] All children in these selected schools got special help in English. The defendants further maintained that no student had an absolute right to bilingual education under federal or state law.[12]

Judge Lloyd H. Burke agreed with the school system. He did not believe that the Chinese youngsters were entitled to more consideration than any other group of children. Although disappointed with the decision, Edward Steinman was not surprised. All along he had suspected the court was leaning toward the defendants, and he had planned for this conclusion.[13] Once the ruling was announced, it had to be officially written up as an order. Although the judge had the sole authority to issue the order, Steinman volunteered to write the statement for his approval. This is an unusual task for the losing lawyer, but Steinman hoped to put his own stamp on the document. In his legal reasoning, Steinman was careful to note Judge Burke's finding that the children could not claim a violation of the Civil Rights Act of 1964. This was a crucial statement. By mentioning the landmark law, Steinman was laying the groundwork for future arguments on appeal.[14]

Appeals

There was never any question in Steinman's mind that the decision should be appealed. When he went to speak with the Chinese families, he said he considered the decision a "temporary setback."[15] Heartened by his determination, Kinney Lau's mother and the other Chinese-American parents signed the documents that would take their case to the next level of court. But for all his confidence, Steinman had a growing sense of urgency. Appealing the decision would be a lengthy procedure. Meanwhile, an entire school year had gone by. In several months Kinney Lau would enter second grade, still not able to speak or understand English.

More than two years passed before the United States

Court of Appeals for the Ninth Circuit reached a decision. The children had lost again. Judge Trask said that it was not the school district's fault that the appellants (those appealing the case) did not speak English. The schools' responsibility went "no further than to provide them with the same facilities, textbooks, teachers, and curriculum as is provided to other children in the district."[16]

But not everyone agreed with this view. Judge Irving Hill expressed a different opinion:

> A small child can profit from his education only when he is able to understand the instruction, ask and answer questions, and speak with his classmates and teachers. When he cannot understand the language employed in the school, he cannot be said to have an educational opportunity in any sense.[17]

In spite of Judge Hill's support for their position, the Chinese children were no closer to getting the English instruction they needed. There was only one place to go—the Supreme Court of the United States. Steinman considered the situation carefully. A loss at the Supreme Court level would be even worse than the two earlier defeats. There was also the possibility that the Court would choose not to consider the case at all. Every year thousands of cases are submitted to the Supreme Court. Only a few are selected for further examination and for oral arguments. The rest are denied a public hearing. But Steinman thought he could beat the odds.[18] Not only did he think he could persuade the Court to accept the case, he thought he could win.

Once again, Steinman contacted the Chinese families involved in the suit. Because many of them did not have telephones, he visited most parents in their homes. Little had changed for these families since the beginning of the lawsuit three years earlier. The oldest children named on the lawsuit, David Leong and Paulette Cheung, were now seventeen years old. A favorable outcome would no longer help them, but would still drastically change the lives of the younger plaintiffs. At nine years old, third-grader Kinney Lau was still not learning English in school. Steinman urged his mother and the other parents to take the case to the highest court in the land.

5

The Case for the Chinese-Speaking Students

By the time the appellate court ruled, Steinman had taken a job teaching law at Santa Clara University. Busy with classes, he had no time to appeal the decision until spring break. The delay was fortunate because, in the meantime, the Supreme Court decided another case that would have a direct effect on how Steinman presented the petitioners' arguments on appeal.[1]

San Antonio School District v. Rodriguez

Steinman studied the Supreme Court's *Rodriguez* ruling carefully. In the summer of 1968, Mexican-American parents had filed a class action suit against a school district in San Antonio, Texas. Several people took the case to court on behalf of a much larger group. The parents objected to the way in which Texas financed schools partly through local property taxes. Wealthy areas where taxes were high generated more funds than did poor neighborhoods. This meant that schools in richer areas had more money to spend. The parents felt this was unfair because students in the lower-income areas did not have all the benefits of the more affluent schools. They argued that the Equal Protection Clause of the Fourteenth Amendment to the Constitution forbids this kind of discrimination. According to the Fourteenth Amendment, no state can "deny to any person within its jurisdiction the equal protection of the laws."[2] Giving some public schools advantages over other public schools was therefore unconstitutional.

The district court agreed with the parents, and the state of Texas appealed to the Supreme Court. On March 21, 1973, the Supreme Court reversed the decision of the lower court. In delivering the opinion of the Court, Justice Lewis Powell pointed out that no one denied that the children in the poorer school were receiving an education. The question was whether they received a poorer quality education—an issue that could not be readily proved. In addition, the Justice declared that "at least where wealth is involved, the Equal Protection Clause does not require absolute equality or precisely equal advantages. . . . Nor, indeed, . . . can any system assure equal quality of education except in the most relative sense."[3]

Reviewing the opinion, Edward Steinman saw at once

that the Supreme Court would not accept some of his arguments in *Lau* v. *Nichols*. Basically, the Justices had said that the courts should not be judging the quality of school programs. "This case was a red light to the federal courts," Steinman recalled. "[They] were not to be surrogate [substitute] school boards."[4]

Despite the *Rodriguez* ruling, Steinman believed he could show the Supreme Court good reason to intervene in the San Francisco School District. On April 9, 1973, he filed for a writ of *certiorari* (also called cert), a formal request for review of the *Lau* case by the Supreme Court. In presenting the case, Steinman decided to include only the first class of plaintiffs from the original lawsuit. He believed that these children, who were getting no English instruction at all, had a very strong claim to legal action. But based on the *Rodriguez* decision, Steinman felt that the second class of plaintiffs, those who got some help with English, would weaken the case.[5] The Court might say these students did get some education after all and decline to get involved. Steinman believed, however, that if he could get the case heard and if he could win, both groups of children would share in the benefits. In the petition for certiorari Steinman concisely explained why the Supreme Court should review the case and asked to have the records sent from the lower court. The Court could either grant certiorari and consider the case or deny Steinman's petition. An unofficial rule, known as the Rule of Four, stipulates that at least four Justices have to vote to review a case in order for it to be accepted.[6]

Lau v. *Nichols* cleared that hurdle. The Supreme Court granted *certiorari* on June 11, 1973, two months after the writ had been filed. Now it was time to draft another important document. With the help of two other lawyers, Clarence Moy and Kenneth Hecht, Steinman began writing the petitioners' brief, a summary of the most important arguments in a case. The brief would explain why the lower court decision should be reversed. It would examine constitutional issues and review past court decisions to show how the principles they established related to the case under consideration. Together, the team of lawyers developed four major arguments to explain why the San Francisco school board should be forced to change its policy.

Chinese-Speaking Children Denied an Education

In the *Rodriguez* case, all the children were receiving at least a minimum education. In contrast, Steinman argued that the Chinese-speaking children in San Francisco were receiving no education at all. The California Education Code had made English the basic language used to teach in public schools. Even though the children sat in a classroom for the required number of hours each day, they could not understand the teachers or read any of the textbooks. "Confinement without rational basis," Steinman described their situation.[7]

Steinman reminded the Court of a statement made by Justice Felix Frankfurter two decades earlier: "[T]here is no greater inequality than the equal treatment of unequals."[8] The Chinese-speaking children were being treated exactly the same as children whose first language was English. But they required different treatment if they were to gain anything from their school experience. Teachers and materials appropriate to the English-speaking children were not appropriate to the petitioners.

To support conclusions that he considered "obvious," Steinman quoted admissions the school district had made in district court: "For [these] children, the lack of English

The interior of the Supreme Court of the United States is shown here. The Court agreed to hear *Lau* v. *Nichols* on June 11, 1973. Now it was up to the lawyers for each side to present their case.

means poor performance in school. The secondary student is almost inevitably doomed to be a dropout and become another unemployable in the ghetto."[9] By denying the children an education, the school board also denied them the chance to hold a good job in the future and to exercise their rights as citizens.

The Equal Protection Clause

The school district's policy had created two separate groups of students. English-speaking young people had the opportunity to learn and develop their potential. Chinese-speaking children did not. Steinman compared this situation to "a hospital administering to all patients the same drug, which is helpful to some patients and harmful to others."[10] This inequality, he claimed, was a violation of rights guaranteed by the Equal Protection Clause. This provision of the Fourteenth Amendment to the Constitution prohibits any state from "deny[ing] to any person within its jurisdiction the equal protection of the laws." But the educational rights of the petitioners were not being protected. It was true that the state of California had not passed laws that prevented the children from learning English. For that reason, the Court of Appeals for the Ninth Circuit had not considered the Fourteenth Amendment in its decision. But Steinman argued that this ruling was wrong. It did not matter whether the state had caused the children's inability to speak English. The students still had rights.

55

According to the petitioners, the Ninth Circuit had misunderstood the difference between "mere superficial equality," which provided the same books and teachers to all students, and true equality, which would meet the specific needs of the Chinese children. The case of *Brown* v. *Board of Education* had made it clear that "surface equality" is not enough and that "education in its essence involves much more than equal books, courses, and desks."[11] To show what he meant, Steinman reviewed two cases that the Court had considered in deciding the *Brown* case. In *Sweatt* v. *Painter*, the Court had ruled that a newly opened, segregated law school did not offer black students the same "creative intellectual life" as did the University of Texas law school that white students attended.[12] The second case, *McLarin* v. *Oklahoma State Regents*, involved a black graduate student who used the same facilities as white students but did not actually attend classes with them. This too was unacceptable to the Court because a learning environment was held to be much more than books and buildings. Denied the right to study and discuss issues with fellow students, the petitioner was also denied important learning opportunities and his constitutional rights under the Fourteenth Amendment.

The precedent, or pattern set by decisions in prior court cases, was clear. Just because students used the same facilities and materials did not mean they were getting an equal education. Steinman pressed his point further with an illustration that did not pertain to schools. He reminded the Court that financially needy individuals who are accused of a crime are given free legal services even though the state did not cause their poverty. Then he reviewed a case in which a Spanish-speaking man on trial in New York was assigned a lawyer who spoke only English. No translator was provided. Later the defendant sued the state because he had not understood the legal proceedings against him. The court of appeals decided in his favor, noting that he "deserved more than to sit in total incomprehension as the trial proceeded."[13] Steinman argued that the Chinese-speaking children had the same right to understand what was going on around them.

The young petitioners and their parents were caught in a bind. On one hand, state law required all children between six and sixteen to attend school. On the other hand, school policy designated English as "the basic language of instruction in all schools."[14] In effect, the petitioners were forced into a situation from which they could not gain any benefits.

Judicial Scrutiny

Throughout American history, certain groups have been treated unfairly. For example, African Americans, American Indians, and Hispanics have had to struggle for their constitutional rights. To fight discrimination, the courts developed a procedure known as judicial scrutiny. To scrutinize something is to study it very carefully. The courts agreed to pay special attention to cases claiming unjust or biased treatment against certain classes of people. These classes are labeled "suspect." The normal legal process is reversed in cases involving judicial scrutiny. Usually the task of proving an accusation falls on the accuser. However, in cases involving judicial scrutiny, it is the defendant who must justify his or her actions.

Steinman argued that the actions of the school district harmed children from a specific ethnic group. The Chinese petitioners were a "suspect" group and entitled to judicial scrutiny. To support this claim of "suspect" status, Steinman tried to prove that historically the Chinese had suffered a good deal of discrimination. He cited two Supreme Court cases in which Chinese individuals claimed unfair treatment. In 1886, in *Wick Wo* v. *Hopkins*, the owner of a San Francisco laundry charged that the unequal enforcement of a city ordinance deprived him of his business simply because he was Chinese. Forty years later, Chinese-speaking merchants in the Philippines claimed discrimination when a law made it illegal to keep financial records in any language but Spanish, English, or a local dialect. In both cases, the Supreme Court found that the laws took unfair advantage of Chinese businesspeople. Their equal protection rights were being denied because of their national origins. Based on the historical record, Steinman concluded that the Chinese-speaking schoolchildren were included in "the special judicial protection accorded 'suspect classes.'"[15]

By claiming "suspect" status for Kinney Lau and similarly affected students, Steinman put the burden of proof on the school district. Officials had to show that they had extremely important or compelling reasons for not teaching the children English or giving them instruction in Chinese. But they had not shown any reasons powerful enough to justify denying a whole category of children an education. After all, as Steinman wrote in the brief, "The school district's purpose in providing public schools is to educate students, not to fail to do so."[16]

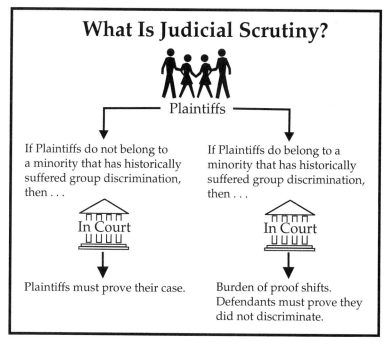

What Is Judicial Scrutiny?

Plaintiffs

If Plaintiffs do not belong to a minority that has historically suffered group discrimination, then . . .

In Court

Plaintiffs must prove their case.

If Plaintiffs do belong to a minority that has historically suffered group discrimination, then . . .

In Court

Burden of proof shifts. Defendants must prove they did not discriminate.

Throughout American history, certain groups have been treated unfairly. To fight discrimination, the courts developed a procedure known as judicial scrutiny. The courts agreed to pay special attention to cases claiming biased treatment.

59

The Civil Rights Act of 1964

In addition to violating the children's rights under the Fourteenth Amendment, Steinman maintained that the school district also defied the Civil Rights Act of 1964. Every year the San Francisco school system received millions of dollars from the federal government.[17] In return, the district had to make sure that all students enjoyed equal opportunities in programs that used these funds. The Department of Health, Education, and Welfare (HEW) had issued strict guidelines to make sure that no student suffered on the basis of "race, color, or national origin."[18] Advisers who studied and interpreted the law knew that language barriers often excluded children of certain "national origins" from participating fully in school life. On July 10, 1970, HEW had published rules that dealt specifically with children who spoke little or no English. Schools were required to take "affirmative steps to rectify the language deficiency to open instructional programs to these students."[19] In other words, the schools had to do something to help the children. They could not provide non-English-speaking children with "mere detention . . . in a classroom from which no educational benefits can be derived."[20] They had to find a way to give all children a meaningful education if they wanted to continue receiving federal funds.

Friends of the Court

Chinese-speaking students and their parents were not the only ones with a strong interest in the outcome of *Lau* v. *Nichols*. If the petitioners won, the legal principles established would affect speakers of other foreign languages. For example, Spanish-speaking children could also claim the right to special English instruction. Hispanic organizations such as the Association of Mexican American Educators and the Puerto Rican Legal Defense and Education Fund wanted to help the petitioners. Although they were not parties in the case, these groups had a way to make their voices heard. As *amici curiae,* or "friends of the court," they were permitted to file briefs. In these statements, they could explain why they believed a decision in favor of the children was important.

There was even a brief filed on behalf of all the Spanish-speaking children in California. About eighty thousand Hispanic young people there did not speak English, but less than half were taught the language.[21] Lawyers for the young Hispanic students wrote *amicus* briefs recounting the educational experiences of several students eager to learn but frustrated in classrooms where the teachers did not speak Spanish. Such children had little to look forward to either in school or as adults. The brief described the situation in stark terms: "To compel a monolingual Spanish-speaking child to sit all day, every day, in a class being taught solely in English, is to impose upon him a life sentence of poverty for the crime of being unable to speak English."[22]

Several important teachers' organizations agreed with the need to teach children English. The National Education Association and California Teachers' Association argued that the appeals court was wrong when it said non-English-speaking children need only be provided with the same books and teachers as everyone else. "If that is so," stated the *amicus curiae* brief,

> it would be permissible to expect blind children to read textbooks they cannot see and to require deaf children to understand lectures they cannot hear as long as the textbooks and lectures were the same as those "provided to other children."[23]

The petitioners had very strong friends on their side, including the United States government. Its *amicus curiae* brief stated bluntly, "By establishing English as the language of instruction and refusing to teach that language to petitioners, [the school district] deprive[s] a large ethnic minority of access to a basic education."[24]

Would the Supreme Court agree that San Francisco schools were not fulfilling their obligation to Chinese-speaking children? The prosecution had built a strong case. Now lawyers for the school system would have a chance to present their own side. One by one, they would dispute the points that Steinman had made. Which side was backed by the law and the Constitution? Only the Supreme Court could decide.

6

The Case for the School District

Lawyers for the school system were quick to maintain that *Lau* v. *Nichols* was "not a case of racial discrimination and should not be viewed as such."[1] Thomas O'Connor, San Francisco's city attorney, worked hard to show that the school district treated all students fairly. Helping him were two deputy city attorneys, George Krueger and Burk Delventhal. The three men had to prove that the children's Fourteenth Amendment rights were not violated and that the school district's programs did comply with the Civil Rights Act. Like the petitioners, they turned to past court decisions to support their decision. Delventhal wrote most of the brief that was presented to the Supreme Court.[2]

Education Is Not a Right

The Chinese petitioners had charged that their rights to an equal and meaningful education were being violated. But according to the school district, no children in San Francisco, California, or, for that matter, the entire country, could demand an education as their legal due. The rights of all American citizens are spelled out in the Constitution. Nowhere in the Constitution was education listed as one of the basic rights of all citizens.

Of course, California, like every other state in the union, realized the importance of well-informed, literate citizens. It did provide free public schools so children would learn the basic skills they needed to function as adults. Education prepared future citizens to support themselves, contribute to society, and fulfill their roles as knowledgeable voters. That was why the state *chose* to establish schools. It was not required to do so. Even though the Chinese-speaking children clearly needed special help, they had no "constitutional right . . . to demand that the school district provide a remedy for their problems."[3] Besides, it was not up to the courts to make educational decisions. Only the state lawmakers had the power to change the way schools should be operated. Although elected officials had permitted local school districts to provide bilingual classes in certain instances, no law required them to do so.

All Aspects of a Problem

State lawmakers had already started to address the problems of non-English-speaking children. The San Francisco Unified School District maintained that it was not required to solve the whole problem at once. The Equal Protection Clause of the Fourteenth Amendment should not be interpreted that way. Quoting another court case, Delventhal argued that the Fourteenth Amendment did not require a state to "choose between attacking every aspect of a problem or not attacking the problem at all."[4] He used the 1969 case *McDonald* v. *Board of Election Commissioners* to make his point. Prisoners awaiting sentence in an Illinois jail claimed their voting rights were violated because they were not allowed to file for absentee ballots as physically disabled people were permitted to do. The Court disagreed, ruling that no one had a right to an absentee ballot. The claimed right to an absentee ballot was not the same as the right to vote. Similarly, the school district asserted that the "claimed right" to special educational programs was not the same as the right to an education. The plaintiffs said that they suffered "precisely such an absolute denial of educational opportunity,"[5] but the school system denied this.

No Compelling State Interest

Steinman and the petitioners maintained that the state had to demonstrate a compelling (forceful and convincing) reason why it should not offer English instruction to the

Chinese-speaking children. They were a suspect category entitled to special protection under the law. Lawyers for the defendants countered that the San Francisco district had not intended to discriminate against the children. In order to qualify for "judicial scrutiny," the plaintiffs had to show that the school district meant to harm them because of their "national origins." The mere fact that the children belonged to an ethnic minority was not enough. Delventhal put it bluntly: "If the defendants had passed a law prohibiting children of Chinese ancestry or Chinese-speaking children who cannot speak English from attending school, then there would be a suspect classification."[6]

Next, the team of defense lawyers refuted the petitioners' readings of the two Supreme Court cases they had used to establish the "suspect classification." *Wick Wo* v. *Hopkins* and *Yu Cong Eng* v. *Trinidad* both involved attempts to segregate the Chinese from the rest of society and to treat them differently.[7] No such intent could be charged in the case of the school district. Its policies were made not to harm the Chinese-speaking children but to meet the needs of the general population. Many Chinese students thrived in the San Francisco public schools. Almost 30 percent of the students at Lowell High School, the city's most elite and rigorous school, were Chinese.[8] This was higher than the percentage of Chinese children in the school district at large. They were admitted to the selective school because of their high grades in junior high.

How could such students succeed if the school district purposefully discriminated against their ethnic group?

No action on the part of the San Francisco school system had caused the petitioners' problem. The reason so many children could not speak English was that more and more people of Chinese origin, who spoke only Chinese, were coming to the United States. The issue was whether the schools should have to solve a problem that they had not created. The district's lawyers argued that some form of forced segregation must exist if the schools were to be held accountable for the situation of the Chinese children. But such segregation would create other problems and violate the students' rights. Far from segregating the students, the district had put them into the same classes as everyone else. This was not what the petitioners wanted. They wanted to be separated on the basis of language and given special treatment.[9] Such an outcome, argued the school system, would not be in the best interests of society. Many other groups exist with "recognized disabilities." The government can not help all of them. But if the petitioners won their case, it might be expected to do so. A win for the petitioners would set an example for other groups to claim their rights were being violated unless the state did something to help them.

Rights Versus Needs

According to the school district, the petitioners had mistaken the words "right" and "need." Certainly Kinney Lau and the other Chinese-speaking children in the district needed to learn English. But because a group has a need does not mean it also has a constitutional right. Courts were created to enforce rights. Needs, however, have to be taken to lawmakers and administrators—not judges. The petitioners had sought help in the wrong place. They should urge their state lawmakers to address the problem. If a law was passed requiring schools to provide English language instruction when necessary, the Chinese-speaking children would have a right. Then they could turn to the courts if that right were denied.

To demonstrate how the process was supposed to work, Delventhal quoted the California Education Code, which had been amended in 1967 and 1968.

> The governing board of any school district may determine when and under what circumstances instruction may be given bilingually.
>
> It is the policy of the state to insure the mastery of English by all pupils in the schools; provided that bilingual instruction may be offered in those situations when such instruction is educationally advantageous [helpful] to the pupils. Bilingual instruction is authorized to the extent that it does not interfere with the systematic, sequential, and regular instruction of all pupils in the English language.[10]

Before 1967, the code had simply stated that English was "the basic language of instruction in all schools." The additions to California's educational laws had come about because citizens had petitioned the lawmakers—not the courts. But the state senators and representatives had left the final decision on bilingual education up to the local school boards. They were *permitted* to offer it; they were not *required* to do so. No one was given the legal right to be schooled in two languages. Each district could decide for itself which programs were most important in its own schools.

The courts could not create a right that had not been established by the lawmakers. The power of government is separated into three branches: legislative, which makes the laws; judicial, which interprets the laws; and executive, which enforces the laws. The defendants argued that "it is not the function of the judiciary to set priorities and, in effect, create rights."[11] The very idea was "dangerous" and "totalitarian."[12]

Differences Between Citizens

The Fourteenth Amendment guarantees every person equal protection under the law. But people come from different backgrounds. They have different abilities and disabilities. Does the Fourteenth Amendment require the state to even out all the differences between people? The defendants did not think so. Delventhal quoted the *Rodriguez* case, which Steinman had studied so carefully before writing the petitioners' brief. In *Rodriguez*, residents of poor neighborhoods had claimed they were discriminated against because their schools had less money than those of wealthier communities. The Supreme Court ruled against them, stating,

> At least where wealth is involved the Equal Protection Clause does not require absolute equality or precisely equal advantages. Nor indeed, in view of the infinite variables [many factors] affecting the educational process, can any system assure equal quality of education except in the most relative sense.[13]

The school system maintained that the petitioners misunderstood the meaning of the *Rodriguez* case. The Supreme Court had partially based its ruling on the fact that all the children in the San Antonio school district were given the chance to learn basic educational skills. Everyone could learn to read, write, and do arithmetic. The children studied science and social studies. Steinman had argued that this was not true for the petitioners. Language barriers prevented them from acquiring even the most primary education. According to Steinman, the *Rodriguez* decision set a precedent that required schools to provide every child with a basic education. The defendants believed there was a difference, however, between education itself and the opportunity to acquire an education. All students in the San Francisco Unified School District were given the same instructional opportunities. If the Chinese-speaking petitioners could not gain any benefits from their time spent in class, that situation was not the fault of the school district, which had nothing to do with their inability to speak English.

The Fourteenth Amendment does not give courts the authority to overrule a school system simply because some students cannot benefit from its programs.

The defendants created an imaginary example to compare to the situation of the Chinese-speaking children. San Francisco operated an extensive system of public transportation. Paraplegics (people who have no feeling in their legs) might well have urgent reasons to travel to different parts of the city. They need to get to their jobs, to doctors' appointments, and to important events. Because a wheelchair could not fit on public buses at that time, paraplegics could claim that city transportation was worthless to them. They might even charge the state had created a "suspect classification" of handicapped individuals. But that did not mean that the city had purposefully set out to discriminate against the disabled. It did not mean the city had to justify decisions made with the well being of the general population in mind. Turning to real situations, the team of lawyers discussed a California Supreme Court case brought by non-English-speaking Hispanic individuals on welfare, a program that provides government funds to the needy. They objected when announcements lowering or ending their payments were sent to them only in English. The Court ruled that the state was doing nothing wrong and that no rights were violated. In another case, native speakers of Spanish wanted the process of obtaining unemployment insurance to be made available in their language. Again, the Court ruled against them. Like the Chinese-speaking petitioners, the Spanish speakers should have brought their problems to their state lawmakers.

Strong Record in Bilingual Education

San Francisco was actively seeking ways to help children who did not speak English. In 1970, the year *Lau* v. *Nichols* was filed in district court, San Francisco was one of only two cities in the nation that had received funds from the federal government to begin a Chinese bilingual program. People around the world had written to the school system asking for more information about the program. Educators had worked hard to write bilingual course materials and train teachers. A Chinese Education Center had also been created with one hundred thousand dollars of the school district's own money.[14] But the district also had some eighteen hundred Spanish-speaking children and seven hundred children who spoke other languages.[15] It could not help everyone with its current resources.

The First Amendment

The Chinese students were limited in their ability to communicate in an English-speaking culture. However, this did not mean their right to free speech was violated. The First Amendment stated that "Congress shall make no law . . . abridging the freedom of speech, or of the press, or of the right of the people peaceably to assemble, and to petition the Government. . . ."[16] The school system had not done any of these things. Maybe it had not taken steps to help all students take the fullest possible advantage of their First Amendment rights, but that was not its role. The school system was doing all that was required of it.

No Violations of the Civil Rights Act

The school district's legal team analyzed the purpose of the Civil Rights Act carefully. Clearly, the team concluded, the act was aimed at preventing measures that denied citizens their rights under the Equal Protection Clause of the Fourteenth Amendment. The school district had already shown that it had not violated the students' equal protection rights. For that reason, it could not be said to have violated the Civil Rights Act either. This interpretation of the Civil Rights Act had been upheld in other court cases. Judge Burke, in district court, had been following legal precedent when he found that the school district did not have to change its policies. Since the Constitution did not hold San Francisco responsible for the petitioners' problem, the school district could not be required to solve it.

But what about HEW regulations requiring schools that received federal funds to eliminate language barriers that kept children from participating fully in school life? The school district's lawyers reasoned that since the district had not violated anyone's Fourteenth Amendment rights, the guidelines to enforce the Civil Rights Act did not apply to its schools. HEW had no power to demand affirmative action when no one's Fourteenth Amendment rights had been denied.

Although the school district was not required by the Constitution to meet the needs of the Chinese-speaking children, administrators were not indifferent as the petitioners had charged. Delventhal summarized their attitude as one of dedication and concern:

> The respondents are committed to quality education for all their students and they submit that they are best able to determine how to provide that quality education and maximize the utility of the public resources available for expenditure in public education.[17]

Soon it would be up to the Supreme Court to decide the issues. Both sides claimed to want what was best for the almost three thousand Chinese-speaking children. Should the schools be doing more or were they doing everything that could be legally expected? Who should set educational priorities—the courts or local school officials? Lawyers for the plaintiffs and defendants had discussed these questions in carefully considered, formal language. But the heart of the case was the daily lives of the youngsters who continued to sit bewildered and bored in the classrooms. Would change come in time for them? Their futures hung in the balance.

7

The Supreme Court Decides

The petitioners had the last word before the Supreme Court heard the case. After reading the respondents' arguments, Edward Steinman wrote a brief refuting (denying the accuracy of) the school district's major points. Once more he stressed that Kinney Lau and the other children received absolutely no benefits from the education they were offered.

Oral Arguments—the Petitioners

On December 10, 1973, the Supreme Court was ready to hear the case. Each side had thirty minutes to explain its position and to answer any questions posed by the Justices. A large clock hung from the ceiling and reminded the speakers of how much time they had left. A lawyer may finish a sentence when time runs out, but that is all.[1]

Edward Steinman was the first to address the Court. Standing behind the lectern facing the Justices at their large wing-shaped bench, he felt a little nervous. Some of the wisest, most experienced legal minds in the country were seated behind that bench. Five years out of law school, Steinman was just getting started in his career. But he had spent most of his time as a lawyer concerned with this case. He had studied, debated, and analyzed. Although the Justices had a wealth of experience and legal knowledge, they could spend only several hours reviewing a particular case before they heard it. Steinman knew he had all the facts and arguments he needed to present the children's case powerfully.[2]

Almost at once, Steinman had to abandon his prepared statement as the Justices interrupted him with questions. This is normal procedure, so Steinman was not surprised when they broke into his remarks. Someone asked if the children should be taught in Chinese. "Oh no," Steinman replied at once. "Our goal is the same announced goal that the school system in the State of California has made."[3] Competency in English was a requirement to graduate from high school in California. The parents of the children wanted them to learn to speak, read, and write English. Steinman did not say how they wanted this done. The method—whether bilingual (using English and a second language), teaching English as a second language (teaching speakers of other native languages how to speak English as a supplement to their native language) or something else entirely—was left up to the school system.

What Steinman *did* demand for Kinney Lau and the other children was that *something* be done. As matters stood, nothing was being done at all. The children were being passed along from grade to grade without learning English or any other subject. "Although the 1800 petitioners and all other students in San Francisco do receive the same materials," Steinman declared, "the pages are blank for these petitioners. The print conveys nothing."[4]

Steinman knew that the decision the Justices made would affect schools all over the country. In fact, so much was at stake that J. Stanley Pottinger, assistant attorney general of the United States, spoke as an *amicus curiae* in support of the children. "This case does go beyond the Chinese-speaking community," Pottinger stated. "It affects the hundreds of thousands of Spanish-speaking children. . . ."[5] Pottinger argued that by accepting federal funds, the school system had already obligated itself to provide meaningful education to everyone. If it did not fulfill this duty, it was not entitled to money from the government.

Oral Arguments—the School District

When the petitioners' half hour was over, Thomas O'Connor, city attorney of San Francisco, stood up to represent the school district. Questioned by the Justices, he was forced to admit that many Chinese-speaking children did not receive special instruction in English. "Well, why are they not getting it?" demanded the Justices.[6] O'Connor replied that there simply was not enough money to meet the individual needs of all the children in the San Francisco district. Children who were deaf, mentally retarded, and disabled also attended city schools. It was up to the school system—not the federal government—to decide who should be helped first and to distribute funds in a way that would do the most good.

"Do you think that if I went to a Chinese school in Peking I would learn something?" asked a Justice.[7]

"I think you would," replied O'Connor.[8] At the

This group portrait of the Justices of the Supreme Court was taken about two years after the *Lau* v. *Nichols* decision. From left to right are: Justice John Stevens, Justice Lewis Powell, Justice Harry Blackmun, Justice William Rehnquist, Justice Thurgood Marshall, Justice William Brennan, Chief Justice Warren Burger, Justice Potter Stewart, and Justice Byron White.

Justice's prompting, O'Connor explained the immersion method, whereby children hear nothing but the language they are trying to learn. Although this was not the best or easiest way to gain mastery of a language, O'Connor believed it did work. American children could learn Chinese that way, and Chinese children could learn English. "No Chinese child is discriminated against," O'Connor told the Justices. "He has the same education as others. He may not be able to benefit by it as much, but it is not up to the HEW to determine what effect this has."[9] In other words, the federal government had no business comparing the progress of two groups of students who received the same education.

The Petitioners' Last Word

Edward Steinman, in his concluding remarks, denied that the immersion method produced results. When one of the Justices offered his opinion that "sooner or later they will learn to communicate, but not very rapidly," Steinman disagreed.[10]

"That is something which is debatable, Your Honor," replied Steinman. "There is no contention by the school system that if they sit in these classes, they will learn."[11]

"That isn't what your colleague there said a little while ago," pointed out one Justice. "He said that it was effective."[12]

"Mr. O'Connor is, I believe, making statements that are not reflected by the record," answered Steinman. "The school system has admitted, even before this law suit was brought, that these students cannot learn, that they are 'inevitably doomed,' that they are frustrated by their inability to understand the regular word."[13]

The Justices Deliberate

Lawyers for the children and for the school district had done everything they could. At 1:47 P.M., Chief Justice Warren Burger proclaimed the case officially "submitted."[14] Now it was up to the Justices to decide the issues.

Deliberations of the Supreme Court are always secret, but the procedure follows a set pattern. The person in charge of the discussions is the Chief Justice. After the Chief Justice opens the discussion and states his or her views, the other Justices speak in order of seniority.[15] Then it is time to vote. A quorum (at least six Justices) must be present before the case is put to a vote. If the votes are evenly split, the decision of the lower court is kept in place. When all nine Justices consider a case, five agreeing votes are required to establish a decision.

Decision Announced

In the case of *Lau* v. *Nichols* the decision was unanimous. On January 21, 1974, the Justices announced that the decision of the lower court was reversed. Kinney Lau and approximately eighteen hundred other children of Chinese ancestry in San Francisco were entitled to an education that fit their specific language needs.

Justice William O. Douglas wrote the official opinion of the court. Central to the Court's reasoning were the following three requirements of the California Education Code: First, English was the basic language used in the classroom. Second, students had to prove they knew English in order to graduate from high school. Finally, all

Weighing the Arguments

Lau

- Chinese speaking children are being denied an education.
- The Equal Protection Clause of the 14th Amendment requires more than "superficial equality."
- The Civil Rights Act of 1964 required schools receiving Federal funds to provide equal opportunity to all students.
- "Judicial Scrutiny" requires added attention to the case.

Nichols

- Education is a privilege, not a right.
- The 14th Amendment does not require the government to eliminate all the differences between people of different backgrounds.
- The school district offered the same education to all students.
- The plaintiffs did not qualify for "judicial scrutiny" and the school district did not create this problem.

The Justices had heard the arguments from both sides in the *Lau* v. *Nichols* case. There were many issues to be considered before issuing a decision.

children between the ages of six and sixteen had to attend school.[16]

Because the Chinese-speaking children were not learning English, they would not be able to graduate from high school even though the law required them to sit in school for ten years. Douglas wrote, "Under these state-imposed standards there is no equality of treatment merely by providing students with the same facilities, textbooks, teachers, and curriculum; for students who do not understand English are effectively foreclosed from any meaningful education."[17] The Justices meant that education is far more than books and buildings. It is sharing knowledge, skills, and ideas. But for Kinney Lau and the other petitioners there was no chance to share anything.

The unanimous *Lau* v. *Nichols* opinion was written by Justice William Douglas. The Court declared that Kinney Lau and approximately eighteen hundred other children of Chinese ancestry in San Francisco were entitled to an education that fit their specific language needs.

In order to profit from their education, students had to know English. Justice Douglas believed this was absurd. To require students to know already what they should be learning in school was "to make a mockery of public education."[18]

Edward Steinman had argued the children's case on two grounds: 1) their equal protection rights were being violated, and 2) the school district had violated the Civil Rights Act of 1964. Douglas explained that the Court had not even considered the equal protection argument. The case was won solely on the basis of the Civil Rights Act. The San Francisco school district simply was not doing what it was supposed to do.[19] Every year it received large amounts of money from the federal government. In return for this financial aid, it had to follow the guidelines issued by HEW to ensure that all children received equal opportunities. It had to guarantee that "students of a particular race, color, or national origin were not denied the opportunity to obtain the education generally obtained by other students in the system."[20] But while other students thrived on arithmetic, science, and reading lessons, Kinney Lau and the petitioners were learning nothing.

It was irrelevant that the school system did not mean to discriminate against them. The Chinese children were being harmed all the same. Justice Douglas summed up the decision: "Simple justice requires that public funds, to which all taxpayers of all races contribute, not be spent in any fashion which encourages, entrenches, subsidizes, or results in racial discrimination."[21]

Other Opinions

Although all the Justices agreed with the decision, several had concerns they wished to share. Justice Potter Stewart wrote a concurring, or agreeing, opinion in which he re-examined the intentions of the San Francisco district. No one said that the school officials wanted the Chinese children to fail. But times had changed, and the schools had not kept up with them. As more Chinese children had enrolled, nothing had been done to provide for them. This was not intentional discrimination; it was neglect. Since the district did not mean to harm the children, Justice Stewart was not certain that San Francisco had violated the Civil Rights Act and forfeited its right to federal funds. However, there was no doubt at all that the school system had violated HEW's guidelines for enforcing the Civil Rights Act. Those guidelines called for "affirmative steps" to make sure that all children understood the language in which they were taught. The school district had taken no such steps.

Justice Stewart asked what he called "the critical question." Did the guidelines overstep the bounds of HEW's authority? The Justice did not think so. He found the regulations to be fair and reasonable. To continue receiving federal money, the school system would have to help the Chinese-speaking youngsters learn English.

Justice Harry Blackmun expressed a different concern in his concurring opinion. He worried that the decision for the petitioners might be applied to other situations inappropriately. "I stress the fact that the children with whom we are concerned here number about 1800," he wrote in his opinion. "This is a very substantial group. . . ." In some schools there might be only four or five, or even only one child who did not speak English. Blackmun did not want the decision in *Lau* v. *Nichols* to be binding in such instances. "For me, numbers are at the

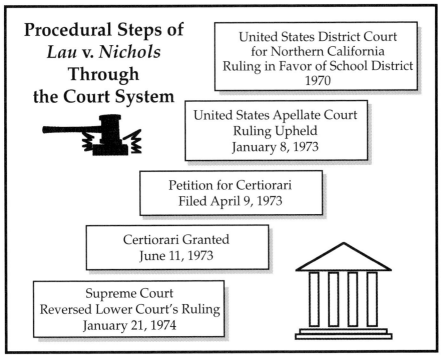

The *Lau* v. *Nichols* case followed a series of important steps before reaching the Supreme Court.

85

Justice Harry Blackmun agreed with the majority decision in *Lau v. Nichols*, but he believed that the number of students affected was the key factor.

heart of this case," he wrote.[22] The Chinese petitioners were entitled to special help because there were so many of them.

Changes Since the Lawsuit

Four years had passed since the original suit had been filed. Fifth grader Kinney Lau and his mother had moved away from San Francisco. Alan Nichols was no longer president of the school board. But their names would always remain on the case that established educational rights for children who did not speak English.

8

Lau v. Nichols Changes Education

Edward Steinman could hardly wait to share the good news with his clients. That night he went to as many houses as he could, congratulating parents on their victory.[1] Now their children had an undisputed claim to learn English in school.

But Steinman had to temper his enthusiasm just as he had once tempered his disappointment at losing in the lower courts. Changes in the school system would not happen immediately. In the suit, petitioners had asked that something be done but they had not said what that something should be. In noting this, the Supreme Court had remanded the case (sent it back) to the district court where it began. There, a suitable remedy, or solution, would be worked out between the school district and the petitioners. Before any new policies took effect, the district court would have to approve them.

Burk Delventhal, deputy attorney for the city of San Francisco, though not anticipating a defeat, was not really surprised by the outcome. He had expected an "uphill battle" in the Supreme Court.[2] School officials were dismayed. They felt they were already doing a great deal to help limited-English-proficiency students. Now the district court would be telling them how to run the schools. Instead of making their own priorities, administrators had to concentrate on the area the court deemed important. They had always maintained they were the most qualified to make decisions affecting thousands of students from all backgrounds. But they would have to restructure their budgets and programs to meet the dictates of the court. "Unfair Demands on City Schools," read a headline in one San Francisco newspaper.[3]

The Bilingual Approach

What kind of agreement would be reached? How would the school lives of the Chinese-speaking children change? Educators all over the country would be watching San Francisco. Many of them hoped to see more bilingual classes created. "It is important that a good program come out of the *Lau v. Nichols* decision," said Lupe Salinas, who worked for the Mexican American Legal Defense and Education Fund in San Antonio, Texas. "It would be a setback [for bilingual education] if a poor plan was implemented."[4]

Ling-Chi Wang, a major force behind the original lawsuit, believed that bilingual-bicultural programs would foster a healthy pride in Chinese-American children. In addition to learning English, they would also learn that their own language and traditions had value. "Nobody should be forced to give up his heritage, his language, his culture," he later told a newspaper reporter.

> By being forced to give up these things, you instill in children self-hate. This is the reason why Asian Americans are so inhibited and withdrawn in the classroom. . . . You visit a playground where kids are speaking Chinese—they are just the opposite, very active.[5]

English Pure and Simple

The associate superintendent of schools, Lane DeLara, did not agree that instruction in two languages was the best way to help the Chinese-speaking students. He favored teaching them English, "pure and simple."[6] That was the quickest and least expensive way to get the children into the "mainstream." Bilingual instruction tended to last longer and cost more money, he said. Besides, what would happen when only four or five children spoke a foreign language? School officials did not think they could offer any kind of bilingual program in those situations.

Edward Steinman, on the other hand, thought there

was enough money in the school system to provide bilingual education to most groups. Funds simply had to be redirected. The Supreme Court had told the district what to do. "And money is not a legal excuse," declared Steinman.[7]

Citizens' Task Force

The school system was under pressure from three sources. There were parents who wanted to help develop the new language programs. There was Judge Burke who called a meeting in district court to discuss how the Supreme Court decision would be fulfilled. And there was the Department of Health, Education, and Welfare, which also wanted to get involved. Government officials knew that whatever happened in San Francisco would set an example for school districts across the country.[8]

Caught between all these forces, the school district agreed to establish a Citizens Task Force. People from all the language groups in San Francisco would get together to discuss what they wanted for the children and how to get it. At the court hearing in May, Judge Burke approved the creation of the task force. He also agreed to let the government participate in the case as it proceeded through the district court. When the Citizens Task Force completed its work, everyone would return to court to see its plan approved.

Parents of Japanese-, Filipino-, Spanish-, and Chinese-speaking children were well represented on the task force.

They spent eight months holding community meetings and working with the Center for Applied Linguistics, which had been hired by the school district to help them. Different minorities had never joined together to solve such a problem before. It was an important first for San Francisco.[9]

The task force called for big changes in school programs for language-minority students. Instead of ESL classes, parents and concerned citizens wanted bilingual-bicultural education.[10] That meant two languages would be used in teaching children with limited English skills. Students would not only learn English, but also gain proficiency in reading and writing their first language. They would study their native culture and traditions and develop a healthy respect for their heritage. The task force thought that English-speaking children could also benefit from learning another language and culture. They were invited to participate in the program, too.

Coming up with an educational plan was just the first step. The task force had to submit its recommendations to the school board for acceptance. Then the school board had to take the plan back to the district court for approval. These steps were not easy because the board and the task force disagreed on important matters, including who had the final authority for the master plan.[11] Hard feelings and harsh words sometimes accompanied the struggles between the two groups. At one point, the superintendent angrily left a meeting, and the task force accused him of "insulting" behavior.[12]

Consent Decree

Meanwhile, the Justice Department was pushing for the establishment of new language programs by the opening of school in 1975. Time was running out. Finally, on March 25, 1975, the school board approved the task force's master plan with a few small changes.[13] One final step remained. The petitioners and the school board had to agree in court. On behalf of the children and their families, the judge had to accept the master plan as a workable solution that would fulfill the demands of the Supreme Court.

Judge Burke of the federal district court still felt that his original ruling was valid and that bilingual education was not legally required.[14] But in accordance with the Supreme Court decision, he approved the school district's plans. A consent decree was issued—that is, a court order that both parties draft and accept. The school system agreed to provide bilingual education, and the petitioners agreed to accept this solution to their problem. San Francisco was now thoroughly committed to providing language-minority children education in their primary languages, as well as in English.

At the Polls

Giving students native-language instruction was an important beginning, but more remained to be done.

What about adults who did not speak or read English fluently? Ordinary things like talking to telephone operators, filling out tax forms, and voting on Election Day were almost impossible for them.

Ling-Chi Wang believed that the language rights gained by the school children could be applied to other situations. He began working with Senator Alan Cranston of California to extend the Voting Rights Act of 1965.[15] This landmark law had enabled more African Americans from the southern states to exercise their voting rights.[16]

In 1975, the Voting Rights Act was expanded to require the use of bilingual ballots in areas with a certain percentage of foreign language speakers. *Lau* v. *Nichols*

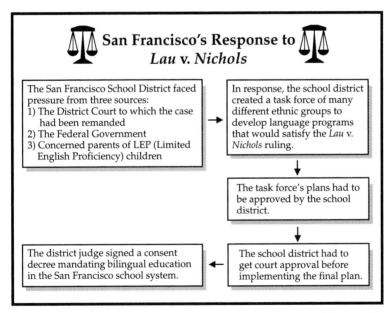

In response to the Supreme Court's decision in *Lau* v. *Nichols*, the San Francisco Unified School District agreed to provide bilingual education.

was cited to strengthen the legal precedent of the new law. Under its provisions, the entire state of California provides ballots in Spanish and English. San Francisco also makes voter materials available in Chinese.

Other Court Cases

Through the Voting Rights Act, election procedures in precincts all over the country were indirectly affected by *Lau* v. *Nichols*. Schools throughout the nation were also affected by the Supreme Court case. Lower courts looked to the decision as a model when questions of language-minority school children arose. In *Serna* v. *Portales*, Spanish-speaking families brought suit against a school district in Texas. Despite the fact that Hispanic children received special help in English, parents did not think their children had the same opportunities as the other students. They felt their children's Fourteenth Amendment Rights were being violated. The court agreed and ordered that a bilingual education program be set up.[17] A similar ruling was made in the case of *Aspira* v. *New York City Board of Education*. (Aspira is a Puerto Rican self-help organization.) In this case, the city schools agreed to offer bilingual education.[18]

These decisions went beyond *Lau* v. *Nichols*. They did not just tell the schools that they had to help the children. They told them exactly how to do so. But one year later, in 1975, a federal court of appeals in Denver, Colorado, declared it was up to the school district—not the courts—

to choose the best ways to help students with limited English proficiency.[19] Building on this decision, another court ruled that bilingual-bicultural education is not a constitutional right.[20]

The Equal Educational Opportunities Act (EEOA)

The courts were sending out different messages. Who should determine the solution when language problems kept children from participating fully in school life? What constitutional rights did these children have? Should the courts be telling schools how to teach? The Supreme Court had declined to resolve these specific issues in *Lau v. Nichols*. Instead it had ruled only on the question of whether the students' rights were being violated.

Lawmakers could not solve all the problems either. In 1974, Congress passed the Equal Educational Opportunities Act (EEOA). One section dealt with the responsibility schools had to help children who did not speak English. But the law did not spell out just what school action was "appropriate . . . to overcome language barriers."[21]

California was willing to go a step further. In 1976, lawmakers passed the Chacon-Moscone Bilingual Education Act, which gave every student in the public school system the right to be taught in a language he or she could understand.[22] When at least fifteen children in an elementary school spoke the same primary language, they were to be enrolled in a bilingual-bicultural program.

Schools were given a little more leeway in dealing with older children, but all students in junior high and high school had to receive a meaningful education—one that was useful and prepared them for the future. The Chacon-Moscone Act placed California in the forefront of state efforts to help LEP children.

The Lau Remedies

While courts ruled and lawmakers set policies, the federal Office for Civil Rights (OCR) had the difficult job of enforcing the *Lau* decision.[23] Were some children still confused because they did not understand the language their teacher spoke? The OCR began studying school districts with large numbers of children who had grown up speaking a foreign language. Investigators found that most of the educational programs to help them did not live up to the standards dictated by *Lau* v. *Nichols.* About three hundred school districts in the country were told to develop new programs for their language minority students and to submit those programs for approval by the OCR.[24]

For some schools this was fairly easy. Other schools faced big problems. For example, the Hillsborough County School District in Florida counted eighteen different languages spoken by students. It had not budgeted any funds for bilingual education. But OCR officials would not accept Hillsborough's proposal for teaching English as a second language. Nothing less than a complete bilingual program would do.[25]

This demand for bilingual education became official in the OCR guidelines known as the *Lau* Remedies. Published on August 11, 1975, these guidelines told school officials how to determine which children needed language help, what to do for them, and what qualifications their teachers should have.[26] If their schools failed to provide bilingual education, they could lose their federal funding. These detailed directives went way beyond the Supreme Court ruling. The Supreme Court had simply ruled that school districts should figure out what to do to provide all limited-English-proficiency children with a meaningful education. Years later, Martin Gerry, who helped write the guidelines, explained why OCR took such a strong position.

> If we had given school systems a choice between bilingual instruction and ESL, they would have all gone to ESL because it was cheaper and politically popular with a lot of people–reasons that had nothing to do with the educational needs of the kids.[27]

Within six years, the Office of Civil Rights helped 359 school districts develop bilingual programs to satisfy its guidelines.[28] Under the new regulations, Alhambra, California, saw especially striking changes in its schools. In 1977, it had no bilingual programs. By 1987, the district had started 120 bilingual classes. Now, while children learned English, they also studied other subjects in their native Cantonese, Mandarin, Vietnamese, or Spanish.[29]

The Pendulum Swings Back

Was bilingual education really the best way to help students learn English and get a good education? The debate continued. Several studies published in the early 1980s suggested that bilingual approaches were not any better than other methods of teaching languages.[30] Some officials who had supported the *Lau* Remedies began to have second thoughts. Maybe bilingual education should not be forced on school districts. Something certainly had to be done to help language-minority students, but the individual school districts should have the freedom to choose their own solutions. Was there really any reason for the government to get involved?[31] It seemed harsh to deny federal money to school systems that preferred different programs to the bilingual approach. Senator S. I. Hayakawa of California summed up the changing attitude. "I believe that given the flexibility to choose their own program, local schools will emphasize English instruction."[32] He believed that immigrant children in bilingual programs sometimes learned English more slowly and took longer to feel comfortable with American customs and society.

Guadalupe Organization, Inc. v. Tempe Elementary School District

Another conflict was in the making. In Tempe, Arizona, parents of American-Indian and Mexican-American children charged that the ESL programs used in the schools were not helping their children enough. They wanted bilingual-bicultural education to be established. When the schools refused to comply, they filed a lawsuit, *Guadalupe Organization, Inc.* v. *Tempe Elementary School District*. But the Ninth Circuit of the United States Court of Appeals ruled that no legal right to bilingual education had been demonstrated.[33] It was up to the schools—not the courts—to decide how best to help children with difficulties in English.[34] The *Lau* decision did not require this solution to all language problems in schools.

Castañeda v. *Pickard*

In 1981, the court was, once again, forced to look at the issue when some Mexican-American children and their parents brought suit against a school district in Texas. In *Castañeda* v. *Pickard*, the plaintiffs accused the schools of racial discrimination in failing to provide equal opportunities for Spanish-speaking children.[35] Part of the parents' complaint was lack of sufficient bilingual programs. The District Court for the Southern District of Texas decided for the school district, and the parents took their case to the court of appeals.

In settling the case, Judge Randall looked to the Equal Educational Opportunities Act (EEOA). Congress had used the words "appropriate action" rather than specifically requiring "bilingual education" in this important law.[36] Judge Randall believed the wording was chosen so that school districts would be free to select their own programs. The act did not require schools to offer bilingual education. However, the judge agreed with parents that the school district was not meeting its obligations. Bilingual teachers did not receive enough training. Their students' progress was not well monitored.

Eventually the *Castañeda* case led to new standards to be used in evaluating special programs for students who spoke little or no English. All language programs 1) had to be based on good teaching principles, 2) had to be well staffed with qualified teachers, and 3) had to be evaluated to make sure that they worked.[37] Future courts would look to these rules in settling other lawsuits.

Teresa P. v. Berkeley

Teresa P. v. *Berkeley* was another milestone case in which the parents of language-minority students tried to prove discrimination against their children. They wanted certified bilingual teachers and better educational materials in Berkeley, California's schools.[38] Once again, the court was being asked to judge the value of a particular school program. The standards set up in the *Castañeda* case gave it a way to do this.[39] In the opinion of the district court, the Berkeley school system had met all three criteria. It did not matter that Berkeley had few specially qualified bilingual teachers. "Good teachers are good teachers, no matter what the educational challenge may be," declared the judge.[40]

The Office of Civil Rights began to weaken its strong

stand on bilingual education. "There is considerable debate among educators about the most effective way to meet the educational needs of language minority students," announced the agency.[41] The OCR would continue to monitor school programs to make sure they complied with the Supreme Court ruling. But different standards would be used. *Lau* v. *Nichols* did not spell out exactly how schools had to help language minority children. As officials allowed school districts greater leeway in

The Nation's Response to *Lau* v. *Nichols*

1974—In the *Lau* v. *Nichols* ruling, the Supreme Court did not tell schools exactly how they had to help LEP children.

1974—The EEOA (Equal Educational Opportunities Act) required schools to help LEP students but also did not say how.

Eventually, the OCR backed down from its firm stand on bilingual education and decided to apply *Castañeda* guidelines to LEP programs.

1975—The OCR (Office of Civil Rights) issued the *Lau* Remedies which obliged schools receiving federal funds to offer bilingual education.

1981—*Castañeda* v. *Pickard* developed standards requiring all language programs to be:
1) Based on sound teaching
2) Staffed by qualified teachers
3) Carefully evaluated

The Supreme Court did not say exactly how limited-English-proficiency students should be helped. So, the debate over whether bilingual education was the best way to help students learn English continued after the *Lau* v. *Nichols* case.

determining what kind of language programs to offer, the *Lau* Remedies developed by the OCR were withdrawn.[42] Instead, the OCR announced that it would use the three-part Castañeda test in reviewing school programs.[43] That would be an acceptable and effective way to uphold the *Lau* decision.

The English Only Movement

Some people felt that too much thought and effort went into the bilingual debate. Previous generations of immigrant children had learned English through the immersion method, they reasoned. Why did today's youngsters need special teachers and classes in their native languages? Such programs kept them from other children. Instead of being separated in their own classes, language-minority children should be playing and learning with English-speaking students.

Some people saw the English language as a sign of national unity. Unlike many earlier citizens, they began to think that being American *did* mean speaking English after all.[44] These promoters of "English Only" wanted to protect the country from what they perceived as the dangers of a bilingual society. Through their efforts, a constitutional amendment to make English the official language of the United States was introduced in 1981.[45]

Although the proposed amendment never came to a vote, the English Only movement continued to gain momentum throughout the 1980s. Looking beyond the schools, the movement's supporters sometimes called for an end to bilingual driving tests, election ballots, and 911 emergency telephone operators. The more extreme members even frowned on McDonald's Spanish menus and television broadcasting in foreign languages.[46]

In November 1986, California voters overwhelmingly

SAMPLE BALLOT
Balota de muestra 選票樣本

Consolidated Presidential Primary Election, March 7, 2000
City and County of San Francisco

1

PRESIDENTE DE LOS ESTADOS UNIDOS **President of the United States** 美國總統		請選一名 **Vote por Uno** **Vote for One**	
AL GORE 艾爾·戈爾		民主黨 DEMOCRATIC DEMÓCRATA	2 →
GEORGE D. WEBER 喬治·韋伯		改革黨 REFORM REFORM	3 →
DONALD J. TRUMP 唐納德·特朗普		改革黨 REFORM REFORM	4 →
JOHN McCAIN 約翰·麥凱恩		共和黨 REPUBLICAN REPUBLICANO	5 →
ROBERT BOWMAN 羅伯特·鮑曼		改革黨 REFORM REFORM	6 →
HARRY BROWNE 哈里·布朗		自由黨 LIBERTARIAN LIBERTARIO	7 →
BILL BRADLEY 比爾·布雷德利		民主黨DEMOCRATIC DEMÓCRATA	8 →
GEORGE W. BUSH 喬治·布殊		共和黨 REPUBLICAN REPUBLICANO	9 →
GARY BAUER 加里·鮑爾		共和黨 REPUBLICAN REPUBLICANO	10 →
STEVE FORBES 史蒂夫·福布斯		共和黨 REPUBLICAN REPUBLICANO	11 →
JOHN B. ANDERSON 約翰·安德森		改革黨 REFORM REFORM	12 →
RALPH NADER 拉爾夫·納德		綠黨 GREEN VERDE	13 →
HOWARD PHILLIPS 霍華德·菲利普斯		美國獨立黨 AMERICAN INDEPENDENT INDEPENDENTE AMERICANO	14 →
CHARLES COLLINS 查爾斯·柯林斯		改革黨 REFORM REFORM	15 →
DAVE LYNN HOLLIST 戴夫·林恩·霍利斯特		自由黨 LIBERTARIAN LIBERTARIO	16 →
LARRY HINES 拉利·海恩斯		自由黨 LIBERTARIAN LIBERTARIO	17 →
JOHN HAGELIN 約翰·哈格林		自然法黨 NATURAL LAW LEY NATURAL	18 →
ORRIN HATCH 奧林·哈奇		共和黨 REPUBLICAN REPUBLICANO	19 →
L. NEIL SMITH 尼爾·史密斯		自由黨 LIBERTARIAN LIBERTARIO	20 →
JOEL KOVEL 喬爾·科維爾		綠黨 GREEN VERDE	21 →
ALAN KEYES 艾倫·凱斯		共和黨 REPUBLICAN REPUBLICANO	22 →
KIP LEE 基普·李		自由黨 LIBERTARIAN LIBERTARIO	23 →
LYNDON LaROUCHE 林登·拉羅治		民主黨 DEMOCRATIC DEMÓCRATA	24 →

p1 001, 011, 021, 002, 012, 022

California voters passed a proposition in 1986 to make English the state's official language. Some people even challenged the publication of voting materials like these, written in several languages.

passed Proposition 63, which made English the state's official language.[47] Although the government continued to provide documents and services in languages other than English, some people challenged the publication of voting materials in other languages. They believed that ballots and legal explanations should not be printed in Spanish and Chinese. California's attorney general dismissed their arguments.

The debate between those who favored bilingual education and those who promoted English continued to arouse strong feelings. In 1987, months after the passage of an English-language proposition, California lawmakers voted to renew the Chacon-Moscone Bilingual Act. But Governor Deukmejian vetoed the bill. He wanted school districts to be able to "fashion their own programs."[48]

The English Plus Movement

Many educators and ethnic groups were upset by increasing efforts to promote English, whose dominance was unquestioned, at the expense of other languages. The English Plus Movement was born in an effort to stem the tide. Acknowledging that all children needed to know English, Osvaldo Soto, president of the new organization declared, "But English is not enough. We don't want a monolingual society. This country was founded on a diversity of language and culture, and we want to preserve that diversity."[49] The battle lines had been drawn.

9

Newest Challenge

In June 1998, voters all over the United States eagerly awaited election results. Bilingual supporters and advocates of the English Only movement were especially eager to know the fate of a controversial proposal on the California ballot. A proposition is a proposed law that is put directly to the voters. Sponsored by businessman Ron Unz, Proposition 227 would require all public school children to be taught in English, no matter what language they spoke at home. Parents and educators knew that the future of bilingual education in the state depended on the outcome.

As the returns rolled in, the votes began to mount in favor of the measure. Soon it was obvious that Proposition 227 had passed. Just twenty years before, bilingual education had been required in California. Now the pendulum had swung back. Bilingual education was essentially banned.

No one denied that the 1.4 million students with limited English skills needed help.[1] No one denied either that the *Lau* v. *Nichols* ruling had to be upheld. The question was how best to help the children and obey the ruling at the same time. Supporters of Proposition 227 believed immersion in English was the fastest, easiest, and least expensive way for children to learn English. Those who favored bilingual education strongly disagreed. They did not want lawmakers telling the schools how children should be taught.

Waivers

Twenty-two years had passed since Judge Burke had issued the consent decree requiring bilingual education in San Francisco. In spite of the new proposition, Judge Burke's court order could not be set aside. Operating under the original consent decree, San Francisco still offers a variety of English Plus bilingual programs and filed reports in the federal court every year.[2]

Some other school districts wanted to continue their bilingual programs too. In California, school officials who believe that a state requirement is not in the best interests of its students can file for a special exception or waiver from that requirement. Even before Proposition 227 passed, school districts in Oakland, Berkeley, and Hayward requested waivers. School officials feared the proposition would succeed, and they wanted their bilingual classes to continue uninterrupted.

When the State Board of Education refused to consider their waiver requests, the school districts filed a complaint in the Alameda County Superior Court. Judge Henry Needham agreed with the school districts and ordered the state boards to review the requests.[3] However, the First District Court of Appeals in San Francisco reversed that order. The justices believed that granting waivers for entire school districts would go against the wishes of the California voters.[4] By the time the ruling was announced in September 1999, at least thirty-eight school districts had tried to obtain waivers.

Even though school districts were unsuccessful in asking for waivers from Proposition 227, individual parents can ask that exceptions be made for their children. Many parents have taken this opportunity to keep their children in bilingual classes. In fact, so many parents had received waivers by April 1999 that Ron Unz felt the school systems were encouraging them.[5]

"We owe an allegiance to our local constituents—and our community wants us to have this [bilingual] program," said Sue Piper, representing Oakland's schools, in which one-third of the children possess limited English skills.[6] The school system sent parents special notices to make sure everyone knew about the right to file for a waiver. If a parent called the bilingual office for more information, he or she could select a recorded message from seven different languages.[7]

Three Men, Three Views

Bilingual education faces an uncertain future in California. Edward Steinman, a law professor at Santa Clara University, is still a strong supporter of bilingual programs. He does, however, expect lawsuits to be filed against districts that offer them. Eleven years after the Supreme Court decision, he recalled that his own father, whose parents came from Russia, started school unable to speak English. "I think there are many, like my father who [learned English] without bilingual education," he reflected. "But the studies show there are hundreds of thousands of people who without bilingual education are not going to learn English."[8]

Burk Delventhal, still with the San Francisco attorney's office, acknowledges the importance of helping language-minority students. "Certainly providing special assistance to students who are not learning is absolutely imperative," he stated.[9] However, Delventhal also believes there are more important factors than bilingual education in determining a child's over-all success. A linguist who speaks four languages, Delventhal feels that "the success of schools depends primarily on the environment at home— the commitment of the parents to education and the respect parents show to education."[10]

On the other hand, Ling-Chi Wang believes that bilingual education is crucial. He hopes to see it expand in spite of Proposition 227. In fact, he would like to see it include every child in the school system. "I believe, in the long run, it is in the best interest of our country to have all citizens to be bilingual," he said recently.[11] "The ability to speak fluently with people from other countries is one that serves every American well." Chairman of the ethnic studies department at the University of California at Berkeley, Wang envisions a system in which all schools offer bilingual programs in several languages. As children enter kindergarten, their parents would choose another language for them to study along with English. "No country has richer and more diverse linguistic resources than the United States," he remarked. Wang wants to see children's linguistic heritage strengthened rather than weakened when they start school.[12]

The Supreme Court spoke out on the issue of addressing the special language needs of public school students. However, bilingual education faces an uncertain future in California. Will the Supreme Court be asked to clarify its position?

Kinney Lau

Most of the children in the *Lau* lawsuit went on to experience the educational benefits that Wang would like to see all students enjoy. After the Supreme Court decision, they were able to learn English and study in their native language. In the lawsuits and regulations that followed, Kinney Lau was all but lost. The Lau family sought privacy and generally refused interviews.

But eleven years after the decision, Kinney Lau spoke to a reporter from *The Washington Post*. A twenty-one-year-old computer-programming student at San Francisco City College, he had learned English and had changed his name to Kenny. He remembered little about the lawsuit and had forgotten Edward Steinman's name. Asked about his early schooling, he replied, "I think the only reason I lost out is because I was lazy. . . ."[13]

But what if Lau had been able to learn in Chinese? Would that have helped his early school performance? "I don't know," replied Lau. He added, "Well, maybe— yeah, it might have made a difference—let's say if I didn't understand something, maybe I could hear a different version of it in Chinese. I don't know. Never happened to me."[14]

Thanks to the lawsuit that bears his name, it *has* happened to other children. Whether the method is bilingual education or something else, *Lau* v. *Nichols* guarantees all children the right to an education they can understand.

Questions for Discussion

1. Imagine you are in a classroom where you cannot understand the teacher's language. How would you feel? Would you learn anything? Can you think of any ways you might try to communicate with the teacher?

2. The First Amendment to the Constitution guarantees everyone freedom of speech. Were the Chinese students' First Amendment rights violated because they were denied the ability to express themselves to their classmates and teachers?

3. Thomas O'Connor, an attorney for the city of San Francisco, argued that "accident of birth" and environmental factors had kept the Chinese children from learning English. He reasoned that if the school district did not cause the children's dilemma, it should not have to fix it. Do you agree with this view? Explain your answer.

4. Edward Steinman reasoned that *Brown* v. *Board of Education*, the 1954 case that required that schools be integrated, spoke directly to the case of the Chinese students. He said that separate buildings were not the only things that separated children from their classmates. Do you agree that language barriers are also a form of segregation? Why or why not?

5. Do you agree that certain groups of people deserve special attention in court because they have been discriminated against in the past? Is this kind of treatment helpful?

6. Supreme Court Justice Harry Blackmun believed that the San Francisco Unified School District owed the Chinese-speaking children special classes because there were so many of them. Do you agree with the Justice that "numbers are at the heart of this case?" Or do you think that special instruction should also be provided if only a few minority language students are involved?

7. What do you think would happen if a constitutional amendment made English the official language? Would the rights of minority-language groups suffer? Explain your answer.

8. Would you like to be bilingual? Do you agree with Ling-Chi Wang that growing up bilingual is a good idea for all children? How might being able to speak and understand two languages fluently affect your future?

Chapter Notes

Chapter 1. Crisis in Chinatown

1. Ling-Chi Wang, "Lau v. Nichols: The Right of Limited-English-Speaking Students," *Amerasia Journal*, fall 1974, vol. 2, no. 2, p. 17.

2. Michael S. H. Chang, "From Marginality to Bimodality: Immigration, Education, and Occupational Change of Chinese Americans, 1940–1980," A Dissertation Submitted to the School of Education and the Committee of Graduate Studies of Stanford University in Partial Fulfillment of the Requirements for the Degree of Doctor of Philosophy, June 1988, p. 92.

3. United States District Court for the Northern District of California, Civil Action No. C-70 627LHB.

4. Ibid.

5. Author interview with Ling-Chi Wang, April 1999.

6. Ibid.

7. Ibid.

8. Tom Wolfe, "The New Yellow Peril," *Esquire*, December 1969, vol. LXXIII, no. 6, p. 196.

9. Ibid.

10. Author interview with Ling-Chi Wang, April 1999.

11. Author interview with Edward Steinman, February 1999.

12. Ibid.

13. Ling-Chi Wang, "Lau v. Nichols: History of a Struggle for Equal and Quality Education," in *The Asian American Educational Experience: A Source Book for Teachers and Students*, Don T. Nakanishi and Tina Yamano Nishida, eds. (New York: Routledge, 1995), p. 59.

14. Meyer Weinberg, *Asian-American Education: Historical Background and Current Realities* (Mahwah, N.J.: Lawrence Erlbaum Associates Publishers, 1997), p. 26.

15. Wang, p. 59.

16. Author interview with Edward Steinman, February 1999.

17. Ibid.

Chapter 2. The Chinese Struggle for Education

1. Meyer Weinberg, *Asian-American Education: Historical Background and Current Realities* (Mahwah, N.J.: Lawrence Erlbaum Associates Publishers, 1997), p. 18.

2. Victor Low, "The Chinese in the San Francisco Public School System: An Historical Study of One Minority Group's Response to Educational Discrimination, 1859–1959," A Dissertation Presented to the Faculty of the School of Education Multicultural Education Program in Partial Fulfillment of the Requirements for the Degree of Doctor of Education, The University of San Francisco, May 1981, p. 63.

3. Ibid., p. 111.

4. Ibid., p. 112.

5. Ibid., p. 134.

6. Constitution of the United States, Fourteenth Amendment.

7. Weinberg, p. 19.

8. Charles M. Wollenberg, "'Yellow Peril' in the Schools," *The Asian American Educational Experience: A Source Book for Teachers and Students*, Don. T. Nakanishi and Tina Yamano Nishida, eds. (New York: Routledge, 1995), p. 4.

9. Low, p. 173.

10. Eric Foner and John A. Garraty, eds., *The Readers' Companion to American History* (Boston: Houghton Mifflin Company, 1991), p. 167.

11. Weinberg, p. 19.

12. Low, pp. 178–179.

13. Ibid., p. 180.

14. Ibid., p. 182.

15. Ibid., pp. 230, 232.

16. Ibid., p. 225.

17. Ibid., pp. 225–226.

18. Ibid., p. 259.

19. Christopher Chow and Russell Leong, "A Pioneer Chinatown Teacher: An Interview with Alice Fong Yu," *Amerasia Journal*, vol. 5, 1979, p. 77.

20. Ibid., pp. 76–77.

21. Ibid., p. 79.

22. Ibid.

Chapter 3. The Beginning of Bilingual Education

1. James Crawford, *Bilingual Education: History, Politics, Theory, and Practice*, 3rd ed. (Los Angeles: Bilingual Educational Services, Inc., 1995), p. 21.

2. William G. Ross, *Forging New Freedoms: Nativism, Education, and the Constitution, 1917–1927* (Lincoln, Nebr.: University of Nebraska Press, 1994), p. 9.

3. Ibid.

4. Eric Foner and John A. Garraty, eds., *The Reader's Companion to American History* (Boston: Houghton Mifflin Company, 1991), p. 316.

5. Crawford, p. 22.

6. Ibid.

7. Ibid., p. 23.

8. Foner and Garraty, p. 360.

9. Ross, p. 14.

10. Crawford, p. 23.

11. Ross, p. 21.

12. Ibid., p. 13.

13. Dennis Barron, *The English-Only Question: An Official Language for Americans?* (New Haven, Conn.: Yale University Press, 1990), p. 109.

14. Ibid.; Francois Grossjean, *Life with Two Languages: An Introduction to Bilingualism* (Cambridge, Mass.: Harvard University Press, 1982), p. 70.

15. Barron, p. 109.

16. Ross, p. 3.

17. *Meyer v. Nebraska*, 262 U.S. 390,398 (1923).

18. Ibid., p. 403.

19. Baron, p. 149.

20. Crawford, p. 29.

21. Ross, p. 20.

22. Grossjean, p. 73.

23. Crawford, pp., 23, 33.

24. Ibid., pp. 31, 33.

25. Ibid., p. 36.

26. Ibid., p. 41.

27. Ibid., p. 42.

28. Betsy Levin, "An Analysis of the Federal Attempt to Regulate Bilingual Education: Protecting Civil rights or Controlling Curriculum?" *Journal of Law and Education*, January 1983, p. 33.

29. *Brown* v. *Board of Education*, 347 U.S. 483 (1954).

30. Title VI of the Civil Rights Act of 1964.

31. Regulations issued by the Department of Health, Education, and Welfare, 1972.

Chapter 4. The Case Takes Shape

1. Author interview with Edward Steinman, February 1999.

2. Ibid.

3. United States District Court for the Northern District of California, Civil Action No. C-70 627LHB, p. 11.

4. Author interview with Edward Steinman, February 1999.

5. Ibid.

6. Author interview with Ling-Chi Wang, April 1999.

7. Civil Action No. C-70 627LHB, p. 22.

8. Ibid., p. 23.

9. Civil Action No. C-70 627LHB, Stipulation—filed May 12, 1970, p. 45.

10. Ibid.

11. United States District Court for the Northern District of California, Civil Action No. C-70 627LHB, Affidavit in Opposition to Motion for Preliminary Injunction and in Support of Motion to Dismiss. Statement of Isadore Pivnick, p. 37.

12. Civil Action No. C-70 627LHB, p. 51.

13. Author interview with Edward Steinman, February 1999.

14. Ibid.

15. Ibid.

16. United States Court of Appeals for the Ninth Circuit, No. 26,155, January 8, 1973, p. 128.

17. Ibid., p. 132.

18. Author interview with Edward Steinman, February 1999.

Chapter 5. The Case for the Chinese-Speaking Students

1. Author interview with Edward Steinman, February 1999.

2. United States Constitution, Fourteenth Amendment.

3. *San Antonio School District* v. *Rodriguez*, 411 U.S. 1, 24 (1973).

4. Interview with Edward Steinman, February 1999.

5. *San Antonio School District* v. *Rodriguez*, 411 U.S. 1, 24 (1973).

6. Ellen Greenberg, *The Supreme Court Explained* (New York: W. W. Norton & Company, 1997), p. 59.

7. *Lau* v. *Nichols*, Supreme Court of the United States, October Term, 1973, No. 72-6520, Brief for the Petitioners, Edward H. Steinman, Clarence Moy, Kenneth Hecht, p. 14.

8. Ibid.

9. Ibid., p. 16.

10. Ibid., p. 22.

11. Ibid., p. 23.

12. Ibid.

13. Ibid., p. 28; from *United States ex. rel. Negron* v. *State of New York*, 434 F. 2d 386 (2d Cir. 1970).

14. Ibid., p. 31; from Cal. Ed. Code - 71.

15. Ibid., p. 39.

16. Ibid., p. 41.

17. Ibid., p. 45.

18. Ibid., p. 46; from United States Department of Health, Education, and Welfare, Office for Civil Rights, "Identification of Discrimination and Denial of Services on the Basis of National Origin," 35 Fed. Reg. 11595. (July 18, 1970).

19. Ibid., p. 47.

20. Ibid., p. 49.

21. *Lau* v. *Nichols*, No. 72-6520, Brief of Efrain Tostado, Et. Al., as *amici curiae*, p. 3.

22. Ibid., pp. 20–21.

23. *Lau* v. *Nichols*, No. 72-6520, Brief for the National Education Association and the California Teachers Association as *amici curiae* in support of the petition for a writ of certiorari to the United States Court of Appeals for the Ninth Circuit, p. 5.

24. *Lau* v. *Nichols*, No. 72-6520, memorandum for the United States as *amicus curiae*.

Chapter 6. The Case for the School District

1. *Lau* v. *Nichols*, No. 72-6520, brief of respondents, Thomas M. O'Connor, George E. Krueger, and Burk Delventhal, p. 2.

2. Author interview with Burk Delventhal, May 1999.

3. *Lau* v. *Nichols*, brief of respondents, p. 14.

4. Ibid., p. 16.

5. Ibid., p. 19.

6. Ibid., p. 21.

7. Ibid., pp. 21–22.

8. Ibid., pp. 23–24.

9. Ibid., p. 37.

10. Ibid., p. 39.

11. Ibid., p. 41.

12. Ibid.

13. *San Antonio School District* v. *Rodriguez* 411 U.S. 1, 24 (1973).

14. *Lau* v. *Nichols*, brief of respondents, p. 50.

15. Ibid., p. 52.

16. United States Constitution, First Amendment.

17. *Lau* v. *Nichols*, brief of respondents, p. 72.

Chapter 7. The Supreme Court Decides

1. Ellen Greenberg, *The Supreme Court Explained* (New York: W. W. Norton and Company, 1997), p. 72.

2. Author interview with Edward Steinman, February 1999.

3. *Lau* v. *Nichols*, No. 72-6520, oral arguments of Edward H. Steinman on behalf of the petitioners, December 10, 1973, p. 8.

4. Ibid., p. 18.

5. Ibid., oral argument of J. Stanley Pottinger on behalf of petitioners, p. 26.

6. Ibid., oral argument of Thomas M. O'Connor on behalf of respondents, p. 38.

7. Ibid., p. 46.

8. Ibid.

9. Ibid., p. 47.

10. *Lau* v. *Nichols*, rebuttal argument of Edward H. Steinman on behalf of petitioners, p. 60.

11. Ibid.

12. Ibid., p. 61.

13. Ibid.

14. Ibid., p. 68.

15. Greenberg, p. 72.

16. *Lau* v. *Nichols*, 414 U.S. 563, 565 (1974).

17. Ibid., p. 566.

18. Ibid.

19. Ibid.

20. Ibid., p. 567.

21. Ibid., p. 569.

22. Ibid., p. 572.

Chapter 8. *Lau* v. *Nichols* Changes Education

1. Author interview with Edward Steinman, February 1999.

2. Author interview with Burk Delventhal, May 1999.

3. "Unfair Demands on City Schools," *The San Francisco Examiner*, January 23, 1974, n.p.

4. Bruce Koon, "San Francisco's Role in Planning Bilingual Study," *The San Francisco Examiner*, May 27, 1974, n.p.

5. Dexter Waugh, "Bilingual Teaching Debate—the Methods in Question," *The San Francisco Examiner*, May 28, 1974, n.p.

6. Dexter Waugh, "Cost Key in Bilingual Programs," *The San Francisco Examiner*, May 31, 1974, n.p.

7. Ibid.

8. Ling-Chi Wang, "History of a Struggle for Equal and Quality Education," in *The Asian American Educational Experience: A Source Book for Teachers and Students* (New York: Routledge, 1995), pp. 69–70.

9. Ibid., p. 72.

10. Ibid., p. 73.

11. Ibid., p. 74.

12. Ibid.

13. Ibid., p. 80.

14. Author interview with Edward Steinman, February 1999.

15. Author interview with Ling-Chi Wang, April 1999.

16. Eric Foner and John A. Garraty, eds., *The Readers' Companion to American History* (Boston: Houghton Mifflin Company, 1991), p. 179.

17. *Serna* v. *Portales Municipal Schools*, 499 F.2d 1147 (1974).

18. Barbara Deane and Perry A. Zirkel, "The Bilingual Education Mandate: It Says Schools Must 'Do Something,' Must Do It Soon—and Probably Must Find the Money to Get It Done," *The American School Board Journal*, July 1976, p. 31.

19. Ibid.

20. Ibid.

21. Kathi Lynne Chestnut, "Supplemental Language Instruction for Students With Limited-English-Speaking Ability: The Relationship between the Right and the Remedy," *Washington University Law Quarterly*, vol. 61, no. 2, 1983, p. 421.

22. Stuart Biegel, "Bilingual Education & Language Rights: The Parameters of the Bilingual Education Debate in California Twenty Years after Lau v. Nichols," *Chicano-Latino Law Review*, vol. 14, winter 1994, pp. 53–54.

23. James Crawford, *Bilingual Education: History, Politics, Theory, and Practice*, 3rd ed. (Los Angeles: Bilingual Educational Services, Inc., 1995), p. 51.

24. Deane and Zirkel, p. 31.

25. Ibid.

26. Crawford, p. 46.

27. Ibid.

28. Ibid., p. 51.

29. Ibid., p. 109.

30. Ibid., p. 54.

31. Ibid.

32. Ibid.

33. *Guadalupe Organization, Inc.* v. *Tempe Elementary School,* 587 F2d 1022 (1978).

34. Chestnut, p. 426.

35. *Castañeda* v. *Pickard,* 648 F2d 989 (1981).

36. Biegel, p. 52.

37. Crawford, p. 59; Stanley Diamond, "Background of Bilingual Education: The Challenge to Local Control in the Berkeley Unified School District," *The Journal of Law and Politics,* vol. VI, no. 3, Spring 1990, p. 584.

38. *Teresa P.* v. *Berkeley Unified School District,* 724 F. Supp. 698 (N.D. Cal. 1989).

39. Crawford, p. 59; Diamond, p. 584.

40. Diamond., p. 585; Crawford, p. 59.

41. Crawford, p. 56; Rachel F. Moran, "Of Democracy, Devaluation, and Bilingual Education," *Creighton Law Review,* vol. 26, no. 1, 1992, p. 268.

42. Diamond, p. 586.

43. Crawford, p. 59.

44. Ibid., p. 65.

45. Ibid., p. 63.

46. Ibid., p. 65.

47. Ibid., p. 62.

48. Biegel, p. 54.

49. Crawford, p. 77.

Chapter 9. Newest Challenge

1. Proposition 227: English Language in Public Schools Initiative Statute, Official Title and Summary Prepared by the Attorney General, voter education material included with sample ballot, California, 1998.

2. Author interview with Jean Ramirez, Acting Director, Bilingual Education Language Academy (BELA), San Francisco Unified School District, May 2000.

3. Bob Egelko, Associated Press, "Court Says Whole Districts Can't Get Bilingual Waivers," *The San Diego Union-Tribune*, September 28, 1999, p. A-4.

4. Anne Marie Stolley and Josh Grossberg, "Court Rules Prop. 227 Waivers Not Allowed," *Los Angeles Daily Journal*, September 28, 1999, p. 3.

5. Ben Wildavsky, "Put a Stop to Bilingual Education? Mañana," *U.S. News and World Report*, April 5, 1999, p. 41.

6. Ibid.

7. Ibid.

8. Cynthia Gorney, "The Suit That Started It All: The Lau Case: When Learning in a Native Tongue Became a Right," *The Washington Post*, July 7, 1985, p. A12.

9. Author interview with Burk Delventhal, May 1999.

10. Ibid.

11. Author interview with Ling-Chi Wang, April 1999.

12. Ibid.

13. Gorney, p. A12.

14. Ibid.

Glossary

amici curiae—"Friends of the court," who are allowed to submit statements or briefs in a lawsuit, although they are not parties in the actual case.

appellant—The party who appeals the verdict of a lower court.

bilingual education—Classroom instruction offered in English and a foreign language.

brief—Concise statement of the plaintiff's or defendant's arguments, or a statement filed by a "friend of the court."

circuit court—One of several judicial jurisdictions in the country that hears cases on appeal from lower courts.

Civil Rights Act of 1964—A law enacted by Congress that denies federal funding to any program that discriminates on the basis of "race, color, or national origin."

class action suit—A legal action brought by a small number of people on behalf of a larger group of people who share their situation.

concurring opinion—A statement written by a judge who agrees with the ruling in a case but wants to address concerns not covered in the majority court opinion.

court order—An official document summarizing the ruling in a court case.

defendant—The party in court who must answer charges.

discovery—The fact-finding phase of a lawsuit in which each side shares pertinent information prior to going to court.

dissenting opinion—A statement written by a judge who disagrees with the majority ruling in a case.

EEOA—Equal Education Opportunities Act, which addressed (among other matters) schools' obligations to help children who did not speak English.

Equal Protection Clause—The portion of the Fourteenth Amendment to the Constitution that forbids discrimination and guarantees all citizens in the United States "equal protection of the laws."

ESL—English as a Second Language, an educational program for children whose first language is not English. Instruction is conducted completely in English.

HEW—Department of Health, Education, and Welfare, now called the Department of Health and Human Services.

immersion method—An educational program in which children learn a language by attending classes that are conducted exclusively in a language other than their own.

judicial scrutiny—A courtroom procedure designed to safeguard the rights of minority groups that have been the victims of frequent discrimination.

***Lau* Remedies**—Guidelines developed by the federal Office of Civil Rights to help schools comply with the *Lau* v. *Nichols* ruling. Eventually, these strict rules calling for bilingual education were phased out.

petitioner—The party who brings a case to the Supreme Court.

plaintiff—The party who brings charges against another party in court.

proposition—A proposed law that is put directly to the voters in a general election.

remand—To send back to a lower court for further investigation or to work out the details of the higher court ruling.

respondent—The party who must answer charges in a Supreme Court case.

suspect classification—A group that has historically faced discrimination and is therefore entitled to special consideration under the law.

writ of *certiorari*—A document that declares that the Supreme Court will consider a case.

Further Reading

Baker, Colin and Sylvia P. Jones. *Encyclopedia of Bilingual Education and Bilingualism.* Clevedon, Great Britain: Multilingual Matters Limited, 1999.

Cardenas, Jose A. *My Spanish Speaking Left Foot.* San Antonio, Tex.: Intercultural Development Research Association, 1997.

Gregory, Eve. *Making Sense of a New World: Learning to Read in a Second Language.* Thousand Oaks, Calif.: Corwin Press, Inc., 1996.

Harlan, Judith. *Bilingualism in the United States: Conflict and Controversy.* Danbury, Conn.: Franklin Watts, 1991.

Romaine, Suzanne. *Bilingualism.* Malden, Mass.: Blackwell Publishers, 1994.

Internet Addresses

Bilingualism:

National Association for Bilingual Education (NABE)
   <http://www.nabe.org/>
American Speech-Language-Hearing Association
"Children and Bilingualism"
   <http://www.kidsource.com/ASHA/bilingual.html>

English Only Movement:

English Language Advocates
   <http://www.elausa.org/>

English as a Second Language:

Association of Teachers of English to Speakers of Other Languages (ATESOL)
   <http://hsc.csu.edu.au/pta/atesol/>

Index